HOW TO DO
just about
ANYTHING IN

Microsoft®
Windows® Vista™

READER'S DIGEST

HOW TO DO just about ANYTHING IN

Microsoft® Windows® Vista™

Published by The Reader's Digest Association Limited
London • New York • Sydney • Montreal

For Reader's Digest

Editor
Caroline Boucher

Art Editor
Conorde Clarke

Sub-editor
Kerensa Leith

Technical Consultant
Tony Rilett

Proofreader
Barry Gage

Index
Marie Lorimer

Reader's Digest General Books

Editorial Director
Julian Browne

Art Director
Anne-Marie Bulat

Head of Book Development
Sarah Bloxham

Managing Editor
Nina Hathway

Picture Resource Manager
Sarah Stewart-Richardson

Pre-press Account Manager
Penelope Grose

Production Controller
Sandra Fuller

Product Production Manager
Claudette Bramble

This Windows Vista edition is based on the Windows XP edition, which was edited, designed and produced by:

Planet Three Publishing Network
Northburgh House,
10 Northburgh Street,
London EC1V 0AT

Acknowledgments

We would like to thank the following individuals and organisations for their assistance in producing this book.

Picture Credits: Pages 61 and 62(bc) – 'Absolute Euphoria', Telstar.

Photography: John Freeman
Software: Microsoft Press Office; Symantec

Contents

Basics

Customising Windows

Windows' Built-in Programs

Good Housekeeping

Troubleshooting

How to use this book

This book makes learning to use Windows both easy and enjoyable. Each task is set out clearly and is accompanied by pictures that show you what you will see on your screen. You'll never be left wondering where to find a command or how to complete a task. And the book includes a wealth of expert advice, tips and inspirational ideas to help you make the most of Windows.

GETTING AROUND THE BOOK

The five sections in this book take you through setting up your PC, mastering Windows activities and keeping your computer in good working order.

Basics

In this introductory section on using Windows Vista, you'll learn how Windows works and how to get around the system quickly and easily. You'll also find out how to save and delete files, and pick up handy tips on organising your work.

Customising Windows

Windows comes with standard settings, but you can adapt these to suit your needs. You can change your Desktop background, create shortcuts to programs and folders you use often, and customise controls to make them more convenient for you to use.

Windows' Built-in Programs

Before you rush out and buy expensive software, try out the programs that are already installed with Windows. These include simple word processors, a basic graphics program and a range of multimedia options for playing CDs or editing movies.

Good Housekeeping

Over time, your PC's hard disk can get filled up with redundant documents and programs. There are also glitches and viruses that can make your computer crash or work much slower than before. Most mishaps are easily solved once you know how. We'll show you how to maintain your hard disk at its optimum capability.

Troubleshooting

Your PC and its software can behave unexpectedly. If this happens to you, there's no need to panic. This section covers common problems and offers easy-to-follow solutions.

WHICH SOFTWARE?

This book assumes that you're using a PC with Windows Vista Home Premium edition. The snapshots of a PC screen are of Windows Vista as it looks after a brand new installation, but four main Desktop icons have been added (see page 12). If the windows and folders look slightly different from those on your screen, don't worry; all the features and tools are exactly the same.

Close up
These project-related tips give further insight into how Windows works.

Bright idea
Make the most of Windows with these inspiring suggestions.

Key word
You'll find handy definitions of technical words or phrases here.

GETTING AROUND THE PAGE

You are guided through the tasks in this book by means of illustrated steps and a range of visual features. Here are the key items you should look for on each page.

Before you start

Step-by-step projects begin with a section of text with points to consider, programs to open and tasks to do before beginning the project.

Snapshots

Pictures of the PC screen – 'snapshots' – show you what you should see on your monitor at the point they appear in the project. Often, more than one snapshot is shown in a step.

Step by step

Projects and tasks are set out in easy-to-follow steps, from the first mouse click to the last. You are told which keyboard and mouse commands to issue, and the programs, folders and menus you need to access.

Magnifications

Snapshots of the PC screen that require special attention are magnified so that you can see them more clearly.

Type in quotes

Quotation marks indicate either the exact words you'll see on your screen, or what you need to type in as part of a step.

Bold type

Any bold text is a command for you to carry out. You might need to select a menu option, a toolbar button, a dialogue box tab, or press a key.

Useful tips

Near the main block of text are explanations of the more complex aspects of a task and alternative ways to do things.

Page turns

The orange arrow indicates that your project continues over the page.

Features

A topic is sometimes presented as a feature, giving lots of general advice and tips, rather than explaining a specific task in a step-by-step format. Often, annotated images will illustrate items of particular importance.

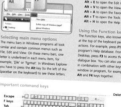

Maximise your disk space

As you create more and more files and install new programs on your PC, your hard disk will start to fill up. If your hard disk gets too full, you will run out of room to install further programs and your PC may slow down. Keep an eye on how much space you have and regularly delete old folders and files to help keep your PC running smoothly.

Quick keyboard commands

Nearly all the actions or commands you perform with your mouse can also be done by pressing 'hot keys' – these are single keys or combinations of keys. For example, you can access the Start menu by pressing the 'Windows' key at the bottom left of your keyboard, or you can open 'Computer' by pressing the 'Windows' and 'E' keys together.

That's amazing!

Items of special interest, and inspiring ideas and explanations, which you can use to enhance the way you work with Windows Vista.

Watch out

These tips warn you of potential difficulties and pitfalls when using Windows Vista, and give helpful advice on how to avoid problems.

Expert advice

Advanced guidance and smart tips on specific features, and advice on how to get professional results with Windows Vista.

Set up your PC safely

When you are choosing a suitable location for your PC, check that there is enough space for all the equipment and an adequate number of mains outlets. You also need to consider lighting and seating, and the surface area of your desk. If you want to connect to the Internet, you will also need to be near a telephone socket unless you have a wireless connection.

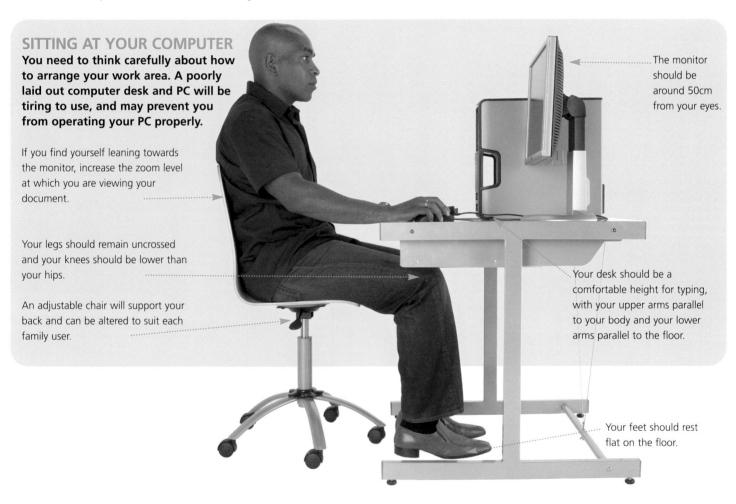

SITTING AT YOUR COMPUTER

You need to think carefully about how to arrange your work area. A poorly laid out computer desk and PC will be tiring to use, and may prevent you from operating your PC properly.

If you find yourself leaning towards the monitor, increase the zoom level at which you are viewing your document.

Your legs should remain uncrossed and your knees should be lower than your hips.

An adjustable chair will support your back and can be altered to suit each family user.

The monitor should be around 50cm from your eyes.

Your desk should be a comfortable height for typing, with your upper arms parallel to your body and your lower arms parallel to the floor.

Your feet should rest flat on the floor.

NAMING AND PLACING PARTS

Your PC's hardware includes all the parts that you can actually see and handle. Knowing how to position these elements ensures a safe and efficient work area.

System unit

This is the part of your computer to which everything is connected. Leave space so that you can plug in the cables easily and to allow for ventilation. Don't leave cables trailing.

Printer

Position your printer near the system unit. Make sure there is sufficient space around it for loading the paper trays.

Monitor

This is the computer's screen. Position your monitor to avoid reflections, but do not face a bright window yourself as this may lead to eyestrain.

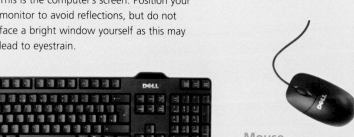

Keyboard

Make sure the keyboard is on a stable and level surface within easy reach. Leave enough space in front of it for hands and wrists. Ensure that the desk is at the correct height.

Speakers

For the best sound quality, speakers should be placed on either side of the monitor and at desk level or higher, not just pushed under the desk.

Mouse

Place the mouse to the side of your keyboard that suits whether you are left or right-handed. Use a mouse mat to create the correct amount of friction, and be sure there is plenty of room to move the mouse around.

Expert advice

If you are planning to use your computer for long periods, either surfing the Internet or preparing your accounts and letters, then you should invest in a good-quality comfortable office chair. Most dining chairs do not offer the support for your back that is vitally important when you are sitting still for long periods. Also, most office chairs are adjustable and so will suit every member of the family. Remember, even with a comfortable chair, you should take regular 10 minute breaks to walk around.

What is Windows?

Your computer uses a piece of software called an 'operating system' in order to run programs and control its hardware. The system used on most PCs is Windows. It provides the connection between the user and the software, and allows the PC to perform tasks, such as printing. Windows Vista, the most recent version of Windows, is fast, reliable, and very easy to use.

SEE ALSO...
- *What you see first* p18
- *Moving around a window* p20
- *Change your settings* p44

WINDOWS

Using Windows is not as difficult as it may seem. The general principles of working with an operating system are easy to learn, and you'll be surprised at how often the same processes crop up, even in different **programs**. In fact, Windows is designed this way – if you know how to open and save a file in one program, you will be able to do it in all Windows programs.

Operating system

The term 'operating system' refers to software that enables the computer's hardware to 'talk' to its programs and its users. While people communicate with words, the computer uses a digital language of electrical 'on' and 'off' pulses.

The operating system translates your key presses, mouse movements and clicks into a binary language of 1s (on) and 0s (off), which the PC's processor can understand and manipulate. Once the task is finished, the results are translated back into a form we can read on the screen.

Quick Desktop tour

If you bought a computer with Windows Vista pre-installed, you may only be able to see the Recycle Bin on your Desktop. However, you can add icons for quick access to other areas of your PC, the Internet and any other computers linked to yours. To do this, right-click on a blank area of the Desktop and choose **Personalize**. Click on **Change desktop icons** from the 'Tasks' pane on the left and, in the Desktop Icon Settings dialogue box that appears, put ticks next to 'Computer', 'User's Files', 'Network', and 'Control Panel'. Then click on **OK**.

Icons can represent physical components, such as your hard disk or a printer, or virtual locations on your hard disk, such as the Recycle Bin or the Documents folder. When you install a new program, a shortcut icon may appear on your Desktop, usually with a small, dark arrow in the corner. To access the program, place the mouse pointer over the icon and double-click.

Start menu

The Start menu contains shortcuts to your PC's software. Click on the **Start** button, then on **All Programs** and you'll see a list of applications. Just click on one, and the program opens. The Start menu enables you to quickly access recently used documents and the programs you use most often. From here, you can also adjust your PC's settings, search for files, browse the Internet and look for help on a variety of topics.

Dialogue boxes

Sometimes Windows and its programs need instructions. When this happens, you use an on-screen dialogue box to make choices – the box may pop up and ask you to confirm or alter an action or it may appear after you click on a menu item or button, offering a range of options to tick or select. One of the most common dialogue boxes appears when you close a file. If you haven't saved since you last made changes to that file, the dialogue box will give you the option to save it before closing.

Key word
A program is software designed to allow the user to carry out a specific task, such as writing a letter or calculating a bank balance. To see which programs are on your PC, click on the Start *button and then on* All Programs.

THE WORLD OF WINDOWS

Every program or file you open is viewed on screen in a 'window' on the surrounding Desktop. Your Desktop may look slightly different from the one shown here, depending on whether you upgraded to Vista or bought a PC with it pre-installed.

Recycle Bin This is where your deleted files are stored, ready for final removal.

User folder Double-click on this icon to open the User window.

User name Displays the user who is currently logged onto your PC.

Frequently used programs The programs you use most often are listed here.

Control Panel Allows you to change your computer's settings.

All Programs Gives you access to all the programs on your PC.

Start button Click here and navigate pop-up menus to access most items on your PC.

Quick Launch bar An area where you can put shortcuts to favourite programs.

Computer Easy access to files and folders in the various drives on your PC.

Title bar Dark when active, light when inactive, this often shows the window's name and icon.

Minimize, Maximize and Restore Minimize (left) reduces a window to a button on the Taskbar. Maximize (centre) expands a window to fill the Desktop; click on this button again to restore a window to its original size. **Close** (right), when red, shuts a window or program.

Search box Type in a file name to search for a lost file on your computer.

Address bar Shows where you are and gives you access to other drives on your PC and Web locations.

Menu bar Lists the series of drop-down menus containing commands.

Windows Sidebar Displays small programs called gadgets, such as a clock, slide show and news feed headlines.

Notification area Change date and time, and set the volume level here.

Program and window buttons The active program button is black. Other programs and minimised windows are grey. Click once to select an item.

Taskbar Contains the **Start** button and useful shortcuts.

Expert advice
If you can't see the Quick Launch Toolbar, right-click on the **Taskbar** and select **Toolbars** followed by **Quick Launch**. A row of icons will appear just to the right of the Start button (see above). You can add your own shortcuts to this area by clicking and dragging. If there isn't room for new icons, right-click on the **Taskbar** and click on **Lock the Taskbar** to remove the tick. Then drag the vertical dotted line to the right. Finally, right-click on the **Taskbar** and select **Lock the Taskbar** again.

Close up
When you double-click on a document to open it, the program in which it was created should open automatically. This means you do not need to open the program separately before you can access the document.

THE WORLD OF WINDOWS

The Windows operating system has been updated many times since it was introduced in 1983. It is now capable of performing a wide array of tasks.

A brief history

The original Microsoft operating system was called MS-DOS (Microsoft – Disk Operating System). To instruct the computer to carry out an action, you typed your commands into a text-only screen. It was successful and reliable but not particularly easy to use, as you had to learn complex instructions for individual actions.

Windows 3.1, released in 1992, used a 'GUI' (Graphical User Interface), which featured simple screen icons and windows. You could point, click on and drag and drop icons with a mouse to give your PC instructions.

The next major upgrades to the system were Windows 95, Windows 98, Me and XP. The most recent version is Windows Vista, which features a new user interface and exciting multimedia features. This new 'look and feel' combines with greater reliability and speed to create the whole Vista experience.

Keep up to date

The Microsoft Corporation work continually on their software to fix problems, or 'bugs', which arise with new versions, and to improve Windows' performance. You can download the latest updates to your current operating system free of charge from the Internet. Just click on

 the **Start** button and select **All programs**, followed by **Windows Update**. This starts your Internet browser program and, once you're connected to the Internet, accesses Microsoft's Web site for information and downloads.

Help and Support

Windows has a useful Help system as well as Troubleshooting features to answer questions, guide you through tasks and help you to solve problems (see page 89). The Help menu, on the right of the Menu bar, offers options relevant to the current program. Help may also appear as a small '?' button on the far right of a window's Title bar. If you click on this, a '?' symbol appears, which stays with the mouse pointer. When you click on an item or command on which you need help, an information box will be displayed.

To open the Help and Support Center, click on the **Start** button and select **Help and Support** from the panel on the right. This displays help

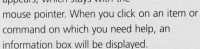 categories and topics, and provides links to the Internet for further help. Certain tasks have 'Wizards' associated with

them, which offer step-by-step instructions in dialogue boxes to guide you through the specific task. Troubleshooting Wizards diagnose and solve technical problems, and can be accessed via Help and Support.

Programs galore

Your PC comes with a variety of programs already installed. There is a basic text editing program called Notepad and a word processor called WordPad. There is also an Address Book, a Calculator and a graphics package called Paint.

Your entire digital library – music, photos, videos and TV – can be found in the Windows Media Center. The Media Player can play CDs and **MP3** files as well as most video formats. You can also listen to your favourite radio station through your computer's speakers using Media Player's Internet Radio Station Finder.

Windows DVD Maker and Windows Movie Maker enable you to import, edit and save your home movies on your computer. If you use a digital camera, transferring your images onto your computer's hard disk is also easier than ever as Windows Vista helps you copy your pictures from a digital camera or a scanner.

Key word

MP3 is short for 'MPEG audio Layer-3'. The term names both the technology involved and the format for compressing audio files. MP3 files are much smaller than the original audio files, yet the sound quality remains high. MP3 files are ideal for use on portable music players and on the Internet.

Watch out

Make sure you buy the correct version of Windows Vista. There is an upgrade from Windows XP or a full version for people who can't upgrade, for example, those with Windows 95 or 98. It is easy to upgrade or install – just put the CD-ROM in your disc drive, and the setup software will do everything else for you. If you are upgrading, you will need your previous Windows CD-ROM.

Basics

You and your computer

A PC is made up of interconnected physical components called 'hardware'. The programs that allow it to perform specific tasks are called 'software'. The operating system is a program that enables the hardware and software to talk to each other and to communicate with the user. It then carries out the commands and displays the results on the monitor.

SEE ALSO...
- *Set up your PC safely p10*
- *What you see first p18*

YOUR COMPUTER

It can be useful to understand how your PC's parts interact.

What's in the box?

Your computer hardware includes:
- RAM (Random Access Memory), which stores information about open documents and programs while the PC is switched on.
- A processor, or 'chip', which acts as the PC's brain, carrying out calculations and operations.
- A hard disk, which stores the operating system, program files and documents that you have created, even when the power is off.
- CD or DVD drive.
- Media card readers.
- Ports, such as USB, jacks for microphone and speakers. There are also adaptors, such as your video card, which provide the connections between hardware and software.

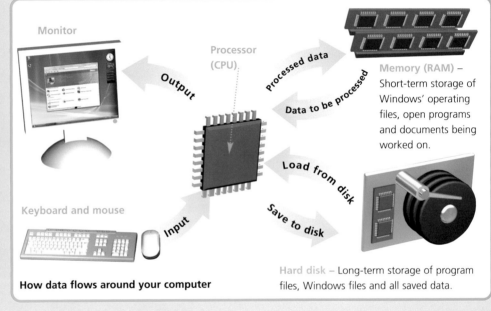

Monitor

Processor (CPU)

Output

Processed data

Data to be processed

Memory (RAM) – Short-term storage of Windows' operating files, open programs and documents being worked on.

Load from disk

Input

Save to disk

Keyboard and mouse

How data flows around your computer

Hard disk – Long-term storage of program files, Windows files and all saved data.

Bright idea
Remember to save your work regularly in case there is a power failure or your computer crashes. This is because RAM is only a temporary form of memory and the data it stores is lost when there is no power supplied to your PC.

The hard disk

This device is the computer's permanent internal storage area. It is made up of double-sided thin circular 'platters' and moving read/write heads. The hard disk stores all data, such as the Windows operating system files, application data, saved documents, your settings and even the way Windows looks on your Desktop. Every time you install a program, alter a program's or Windows' settings, or save a file, some data on the hard disk is rewritten.

RAM

Random Access Memory (RAM) is your PC's memory – a temporary electronic storage space for digital data while your PC is switched on. Data stored in RAM can be accessed much more quickly than if it was on the hard disk, and this allows your PC to work faster. The Windows Vista recommended requirement for RAM is 512MB. However, 1GB will make your PC run more quickly.

Units of data storage

The smallest amount of information that can be stored on a hard disk or in RAM is a 'bit' (short for **b**inary dig**it**). Eight bits make up a 'byte' (**b**inar**y te**rm), which is enough space to store a letter or a number. You may hear 'Kilobyte' (KB) used as a measure of storage. This equals 1024 bytes. Note that Kilobit (Kb) is used for data rates, for example in describing modem speeds. A 'Megabyte' (MB) is equal to 1024 Kilobytes, and a 'Gigabyte' (GB) equals 1024 Megabytes.

The processor

Sometimes called a microprocessor or CPU (Central Processing Unit), this is the brains of the PC. It carries out the calculations that allow the computer to work. The processor performs millions of calculations every second. Processor speed is measured in hertz (Hz). A 3GHz (gigahertz) processor works faster than one with a speed of 900MHz (megahertz).

Motherboard

All hardware is housed on, or connected to, the motherboard, which is your PC's main circuit board. External hardware, such as your printer and monitor, is connected to it via cables. The mouse and keyboard can be connected by cables or by a wireless connection.

The mouse

Desktop PCs come with a mouse as one of the main 'input devices' (laptops usually have a rectangular 'touch pad'). When you move the mouse, the mouse pointer on the screen moves in the same relative direction – you use it to point to and select objects on screen, to open folders and documents, and to issue commands by clicking on-screen buttons.

A basic mouse has two buttons – the left one is used the most. A single click of the left mouse button on an icon, file or folder will select or highlight it. Any of these items can be activated or opened by a double-click (two quick clicks without moving the mouse). A single click on a button, a link on a Web

site, or a menu item will activate it. Clicking some items once with the right mouse button (it never needs to be double-clicked) activates a pop-up menu giving access to shortcuts and extra functions relating to that item. Your mouse will probably have a small wheel between the two buttons. By rolling this wheel forward or backward you can scroll down or across a window rather than using the scroll bars. You can usually customise the mouse wheel to perform an action, such as a double-click, when it is pressed.

The keyboard

Apart from using the keyboard to type in text, you can also use it to do almost everything the mouse does. You can scroll through windows using the up and down arrows and there are many 'hot keys' that are shortcuts to menu or toolbar commands.

Close up
If your mouse is at the edge of the mat but the cursor isn't where you want it to be on the screen, lift the mouse up to move it to the middle of the mat. The cursor only moves when the base of the mouse moves across a surface.

What you see first

Every Windows operation takes place on the 'Desktop'. This is a virtual workspace from which you can access all the programs and files on your PC. You can choose what to place on the Desktop, either filling it with shortcut icons to your frequently used programs and folders, or leaving it free of clutter as a colourful backdrop to your work.

SEE ALSO...
- *Using the Start menu* p22
- *Personalise your Desktop* p42
- *Create your own shortcuts* p50

THE DESKTOP WINDOW

There are four main areas on the Desktop: the Taskbar (and its elements); the Desktop (background); Desktop icons and the Sidebar.

Taskbar

Running along the bottom of the Desktop screen, the Taskbar contains the Start button and Quick Launch Toolbar (see page 13) on the left, and the 'notification area' on the far right. As you open new windows, they will appear as buttons on the Taskbar. You can reduce, or 'minimise', a window on the Desktop to a button on the Taskbar so that you can see other items. To do this, simply click on the – button (left) near the top right-hand corner of a window. To view the window again, click on its associated button on the Taskbar and it will be restored.

Start button

Located on the left of the Taskbar, this button opens a menu, which gives access to programs and other facilities on your PC.

Quick Launch Toolbar

This toolbar allows you to 'launch' programs with a single mouse click but it may be hidden, depending on how Windows is set up. If it is not already displayed, follow the instructions on page 13 to view it. You can also drag icons here to make shortcuts.

Notification area

This holds a variety of useful icons, depending on what software and utilities are installed. The permanent ones are Volume Control and the Clock. Any extra items not in use are hidden, but can be viewed by clicking on the arrow button, to their left.

Sidebar

A long vertical bar displayed on the right of your Desktop. It contains mini-programs called 'gadgets'. By default it displays a clock, news feed headlines and a slide show. You can add additional gadgets, such as a weather report, to the Sidebar (see panel below).

Close up
You can have the Taskbar hide itself automatically when you don't need it. Right-click on the Taskbar and choose Properties. Put a tick next to 'Auto-hide the taskbar' and click on OK. To see the Taskbar again, just move your mouse pointer to the bottom of the screen and it will pop up.

Adding gadgets

To add a new gadget to your Sidebar, move your mouse to the top of the bar and click on the '**+**'. To add, say, the Weather gadget, right-click on it and click on **Add** in the pop-up menu. To customise it (to change the location on the weather report, for example), right-click on the gadget and select **Options**. Type in the location you want and click on **OK**.

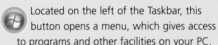

YOUR DESKTOP

If you have a new PC or have installed Windows Vista from scratch, you may only be able to see the Recycle Bin icon. Follow the instructions on page 12 to display the icons shown below.

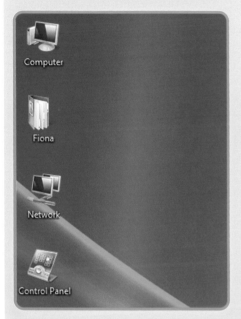

Desktop icons

These icons give you quick access to important areas on your hard disk, networked PCs and the Control Panel. You can add extra shortcuts to the Desktop for any important files and folders (see page 50), but it's a good idea not to let it get too cluttered. To access a feature represented by an icon, place your mouse pointer on it and double-click with the left button. The standard Desktop icons associated with Vista are featured below.

Computer

You can open all the drives on your computer from this icon, including the hard drive, a CD or DVD drive. You can then access all of the files and folders inside them by double-clicking on the icons.

User's Files

Each user – here Fiona – has his or her own folder. To access it, double-click on the folder icon or click on the Start button and then on 'Fiona'. This is the default location in which Windows will suggest you save your files, in various dedicated folders.

To make it work more efficiently for you, learn how to create folders within folders (see page 31). Windows may automatically create folders for you, depending on the Windows software you use: Music is used by Media Player to store your MP3 and other music files; Pictures is for your images from a scanner or digital camera; and Downloads stores files you have downloaded from the Internet.

Network

If your computer is on a network – for example, you may have two or more PCs in your home linked by a communications cable – you can 'see' and access them through this facility. You can then share and transfer files between them, and even share a printer or modem.

Control Panel

Use the Control Panel to make changes to the Windows settings, including the colour and appearance of your Desktop and windows, hardware and software setup and configuration, and security.

Recycle Bin

Drag documents into the bin when you have no more use for them. They are stored here until you empty the bin. This allows you to make a final check before you delete them or to bring them back into use.

Bright idea
You can move icons on the Desktop anywhere you want them. By default, they should 'snap' to an invisible grid. If they don't do this, right-click on a blank area of the Desktop, select View *and put a tick next to 'Align to Grid'.*

Expert advice
Depending on whether you upgraded to or installed Windows Vista, your Desktop, its icons and the Taskbar may look slightly different from the images in this book. However, they should all work in the same way.

Moving around a window

The Explorer window that appears when you double-click on a disk or folder icon provides you with a number of options. Most importantly, it displays the contents of the disk or folder you opened and allows you to open files contained within it. It also gives access to some key functions with just one click, and presents some quick navigation routes.

SEE ALSO...
- *Using Windows Explorer p24*
- *Arranging windows p26*
- *Change your settings p44*

A TYPICAL WINDOW

Double-clicking on a Windows folder will open a standard window which has several key elements.

The Title bar area

This is the pale coloured area at the top of a window, above the address bar (see page 21). Depending what you are viewing, it may display the name of the program along with the name of the document – at other times, this area may remain blank. The colour of the Windows border running along the top of the Title bar

indicates whether the window is active (dark shading) or not (light shading). The shading changes are subtle, but the 'Close' button provides another indicator – if its background is red, the window is active.

You can only work within an active window – to activate an inactive window, just click on it. To move a window to see and access other items on the Desktop, click on the Title bar area at the top of the window and, keeping the left mouse button pressed, drag the window. To

 refresh the contents of a window click on the up and down arrow icon to the right of the Address bar.

Sizing buttons

At the top right of a window, three icons allow

 you to minimise, maximise, restore and close the window. Click on the **Minimize** button

to hide the window. It becomes a button on the Taskbar at the bottom of the screen. To view the window again, just click once on that

 Taskbar button. Clicking on the **Maximize** button enlarges the window to fill the entire screen, and the border becomes black.

 After this, the button changes from a single square to two overlapping squares, becoming

 the **Restore Down** button. Click on it to return the window to its previous size. On the far right, you can click on the **Close** button to shut the window or quit the program.

If you have been working on a document or file and have not saved your work since making some changes, the computer will ask you if you want to save the file before it allows the program to close.

Bright idea
You can maximise a window or restore it to its original size quickly by double-clicking on the window's Title bar.

Watch out
When a program is minimised, a common mistake is to restart the program to see it. However, this will result in two versions of the program running at the same time. To restore a program window once it has been minimised, click once on its button on the Taskbar.

WITHIN THE WINDOW

Navigating icons and menus is easy once you know what options are available and where to find them.

Menu bar

The Menu bar displays a series of words that are headings for drop-down menus, each of which lists related commands. Click on a

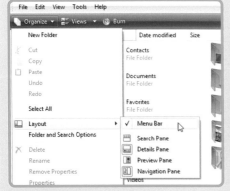

heading to view the menu. If this bar is not visible, click on the **Organize** button, go to **Layout** and then select **Menu Bar**.

Address bar

The Address bar at the top of each folder view displays the current folder address as a set of names separated by

arrows, and offers a way to navigate between folders. To select a sub-folder in the Address bar, click on the right-pointing arrow to the right of that folder. Click on one of the sub-folders to open it instead of the current folder.

The 'Back' and 'Forward' arrow buttons to the left of the Address bar let you cycle through windows you have viewed and the downward pointing button to the right of these displays the previous folders viewed. If the current folder

is in the list, it will be highlighted in bold. Click in the empty space to the right of the names in the Address bar to reveal the full folder path. If you want to refresh the display click on the 'up and down' arrow button to the right of the Address bar.

Navigation pane

The 'Navigation' pane at the left of a folder or drive window includes links to drives, folders, favourites, and other related tasks depending on what is selected within the window. Click on a folder in the 'Navigation' pane on the left to reveal its contents in the pane on the right.

Details Pane

The 'Details Pane' at the bottom of a window displays information about the selected item in the panes above.

Borders and scroll bars

These frame the window, enabling you to resize or scroll around within it. When you place the cursor on the border of a window, it changes to a two-headed arrow. At this point, click and drag to resize the window. Doing this at a corner allows you to resize the width and the height of the window together. Move around the screen to the left and right or up and down by clicking on the appropriate arrows on the scroll bars. Alternatively, click and drag the light blue scroll box in the desired direction.

Change the display

Click on the **Views** button on the toolbar to change how the contents of a folder is displayed. Each time you click on the button, the contents of the selected folder is viewed using the next view in the sequence: by Icon, List, Details and Tiles. Click on the downward pointing arrow to the right of the Views button for extra viewing options (Extra Large, Large, Medium and Small icons).

Close up
If you are not sure what a button on a toolbar represents, try letting your mouse pointer hover over it for a second. A small 'ToolTip' message will then appear showing the button's name, providing a useful hint.

Close up
The Views button allows you to choose how to display the contents of a folder: Icon displays the files as icons with no file information; List displays the files as tiny icons in list form; Details lists information such as a file's size and creation date; and Tiles displays files as large icons with the file type and size.

Using the Start menu

The Start button is a fast way to access the key programs, documents and files on your PC. By default, it is located in the bottom left-hand corner of the screen. Click on it once to open the Start menu, and then select an item, such as 'Internet Explorer', to launch it. The All Programs arrow displays further submenus, containing entries for all the programs on your PC.

SEE ALSO...
- *Personalise your Desktop p42*
- *Change your settings p44*
- *User Accounts p46*

START MENU BASICS

From the Start button you are only ever a couple of clicks away from all the programs and files on your computer.

 Click on the large black arrow to the left of All Programs to open a submenu. Here you'll see a list of the programs on your PC. Often you'll see a smaller arrow next to an item, such as Accessories. Click on the item to see its submenu. Above All Programs is a quick-access list of your most recently used programs as well as icons for the Internet and e-mail.

 Select **Recent Items** to view a submenu of the last 15 files you worked on. Click on one to open the document in the program that created it.

 Click on **Control Panel** to adjust your computer's settings, such as Date and Time, Sounds and Display.

 **Default Programs** changes the default program Windows uses to open certain files such as pictures.

 **Help and Support** has a searchable index of advice. You will require Internet access for some information.

 Select **Search** to find files on your PC. See page 36 to learn how to use the search function.

 The circled button sends your PC into 'Power Save'; the 'Lock' button secures your PC, requiring a password to 'unlock' it. The arrow gives additional 'Turn Off' options (see opposite).

Close up
If you can't see the 'Recent Items' icon on your Start menu, right-click on the Taskbar and choose *Properties*. **Then click on the** *Start Menu* **tab and put a tick next to 'Store and display a list of recently opened files'.**

A CLOSER LOOK

Familiarise yourself with the 'Turn Off' option, customise your Start menu and learn how to use 'paths'.

Shutting down your PC options

Click on the **Start** button and select the button on the far right at the bottom of the black panel. There are six options to choose from:

Switch User – use this to select a different user from the Welcome screen, without logging off.

Log Off – use this when you have finished using the PC but don't want to shut it down.

Lock is the same as clicking on the 'padlock' button. The Welcome screen will appear and a password must be entered for you to return to your account.

Restart closes down your computer and then restarts it. This is useful after new programs have been installed, or if you are experiencing glitches.

Sleep puts your PC to 'sleep' to save power. Move the mouse or press a key to 'wake' it up.

Shut Down closes all programs, saves Windows' settings and turns off the PC.

Customise the Start menu

To alter the Start menu so that it meets your needs, right-click on a blank section of the Taskbar and select **Properties** from the pop-up menu. Click on the **Start Menu** tab and then click on the **Customize** button.

Scroll through the items to customise in the main panel, checking and unchecking them as you go. Select from the options under each

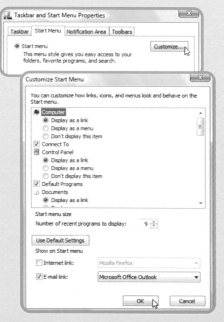

heading for how you want to display that item. Below, choose the number of program icons that will be visible and whether you wish to have Internet and e-mail links shown at the top of the Start menu.

If, for instance, you want to add a submenu to the Control Panel, click on 'Display as a menu'. When you're finished, click on **OK** to close the Customize Start Menu dialogue box and then on **OK** again to close the Properties dialogue box.

If you want to know more about customising the Start Menu, click on the link at the bottom of the Taskbar and Start Menu Properties dialogue box. You will then be presented with the 'Help and Support' page 'Customize the Start menu'. Click on the blue links for more information.

Use the Run feature

By selecting **Run**, you can launch anything you have on your PC, including programs, CDs and DVDs. To use it, open Taskbar and Start Menu Properties as before, scroll through the list and click on **Run command**, then on **OK**.

If you already know where the item you want to launch is stored on your computer, you can type in the route to the file, known as the 'path', and then click on **OK**. For instance, the path to the program WinZip might be 'C:\Users\ Fiona/ Downloads\winzip111.exe'. 'C:' is the drive that WinZip is on, while 'Downloads' is the folder in which it is stored. If you don't know the path to the file you want to open, click on the **Browse** button to search your computer for it.

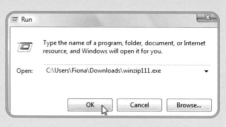

Bright idea
If you want to add a frequently used program to the top section of the Start menu, drag it from its program menu to the Start *button and then up to the required position.*

Using Windows Explorer

Unlike some earlier versions of Windows, the tools and features of Windows Explorer appear every time you open a folder or double-click on a disk drive in Windows Vista. This facility allows you to access your file and folder system easily and efficiently, and also helps you to organise and sort the files in a way that suits your needs.

SEE ALSO...
- *File your work p30*
- *Finding files p36*

FINDING YOUR WAY AROUND

To access the Windows Explorer tools, click on the Start menu and choose Documents. Then click on the Organize button on the Toolbar.

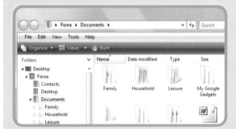

What you see

A typical Explorer window is divided into two panes. On the left-hand side is a list of the drives and folders on your PC. When you click on one of these, the files and folders it contains

are displayed in the right-hand pane. This means that you can search through the entire contents of your computer in a single window.

The left-hand pane is for navigating around your computer. Click on the open triangle to the left of a drive or a folder to expand the contents of that drive or folder. Click on the black triangle to collapse the contents again. This makes it much easier to scroll through the list when you're looking for your files. If there is no triangle, that folder contains only files, which are

displayed in the right-hand pane. Click on a folder or file in the right-hand pane and a summarised description of that selected item will appear in the bottom of the window. The summary will tell you what the item is, when it was last modified, its size and, if it is a file, the name of the author. If you do not see this detail, click on the **Organize** button, scroll down to **Layout** and click on **Details Pane**.

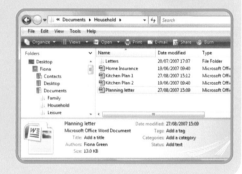

Bright idea
If you regularly work on the same file, right-click on it in any folder window and select Send To, *then* Desktop (create shortcut). *This places a shortcut icon on the Desktop which, when double-clicked, will open your file.*

LOOKING CLOSER

When you are familiar with Windows Explorer, it is easy to navigate your hard disk and reorganise your files.

Sorting files and folders

There are four main ways to view the data on the right-hand side of the Explorer window: by Icon (Extra Large, Large, Medium and Small), List, Details and Tiles. To select an option, click on the **View** menu or click on the **Views** button on the toolbar (see page 21 for information). Select **Details** for the most comprehensive viewing option – you'll see the file name, size and type, and the date and time

it was last saved. No matter how you choose to view your files and folders, you can alter the order in which they are displayed. Click on the **View** menu and then **Sort by**. The submenu gives you several options:
Name displays files in alphabetical order, with the folders grouped together at the top or

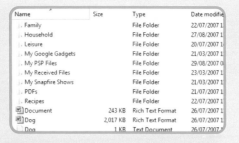

bottom of the list. In all cases, the order can be changed by clicking on the small arrow to the right of the column name.
Size arranges folders by name in ascending alphabetical order, and then files by size, with the smallest file first.
Type groups files of the same kind – such as graphics files or Word documents – in ascending alphabetical order. Folders are placed at the bottom of the list.
Date modified sorts folders and files with the most recently modified files at the top.

Two further options are **Group By** which organises your files in like groups according to the submenu option you choose; and **Stack By**. If you then choose **Name** from the submenu, they are categorised into alphabetical groups, A–H, I–P and Q–Z.

Changing views

If you choose the Details view and have not selected the Show in Groups option, you'll see that the sort order is indicated by a small arrow beside the column heading. You can sort your files by a different category by clicking on a

column heading in the Name bar. Clicking on the heading again reverses the sort order.

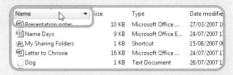

Organising your work

Folders are a good way to group your files together. To create a new folder, choose where you want it to go by clicking once on the appropriate folder or drive icon in the left-hand pane of Explorer. Now click on the **File** menu and select **New**, then **Folder**. A new folder

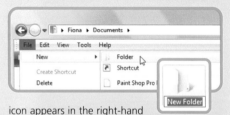

icon appears in the right-hand pane with the name 'New Folder' highlighted. Type a folder name and press **Return**. You can now drag and drop files into this folder. In the right pane, locate the file you want to put in the new folder. Then find your folder in the left pane, by opening other folders until you can see it. Don't click on the folder you want. Click on the file on the right and drag it onto your folder's icon on the left. When the folder is highlighted, release the mouse button to complete the action.

Customising folders

You can change the appearance of folders in Windows Explorer to help identify files belonging to different users. Open the folder you want to change. Click on the **View** menu and select **Customize This Folder**. You can choose a picture to go on your folder, or change the icon to make it more recognisable. The picture will not be visible in the List or Details views though.

Arranging windows

The Windows Desktop can easily become filled with open program and folder windows – for example, a letter in progress, your e-mail Inbox, or a spreadsheet of monthly expenses. However, with a little organisation, you can resize and switch between windows quickly and easily, and still stay focused on the task in hand.

SEE ALSO...
- *Using the Start menu p22*
- *Using Windows Explorer p24*
- *Create your own shortcuts p50*

BEFORE YOU START
Open up a few windows on your Desktop, such as a letter, an e-mail program, and your Documents folder. You can then experiment as you go through the steps.

1 If you need to move an open window on your screen – so you can see it while working in another window, for instance – click on the **Title bar** at the top of the window and drag it across to wherever you would like it. If your windows are the wrong size, you can resize them by clicking on any of the corners or sides; the mouse pointer turns into a double-headed arrow and you can then drag windows inwards or outwards to the new size.

2 The easiest way to work with multiple windows is to have only one of them visible at a time. If there are any windows you are not using, click on their **Minimize** buttons (in the upper right-hand corner).

Each minimised window is shown as a button on the Taskbar. If six or more files are open in the same program, their Taskbar buttons will be reduced to one button with the number of windows on it. Click on it and a list pops up.

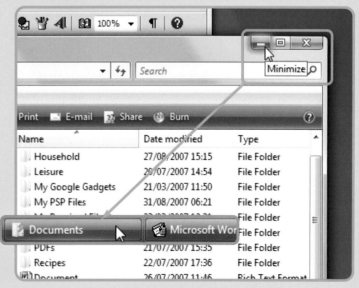

Customise your Taskbar

You can move your Taskbar to the sides or top of your screen. Click on the **Taskbar** near, but not on, the Start button, and drag it to where you want. To make the Taskbar bigger, position the mouse on the line between the top of the Taskbar and the Desktop (left). When it changes into a double-headed arrow, click and drag the **Taskbar** upwards. Note, you need to unlock the Taskbar first, see page 13.

That's amazing!

Right-click on the **Taskbar** and select **Toolbars** to choose from a range of options. You can convert your Desktop icons to buttons on the Taskbar, show an Address bar for Web addresses, or even display a list of Internet links.

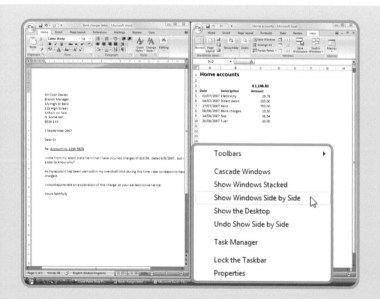

4 If you have three or more windows open, right-click on the **Taskbar** and select **Cascade Windows**. This makes the windows overlap slightly so you can view all the Title bars

at once (below). Or, to clear the Desktop of all windows, click on the **Show the Desktop** button and all the windows will instantly be reduced to buttons on your Taskbar.

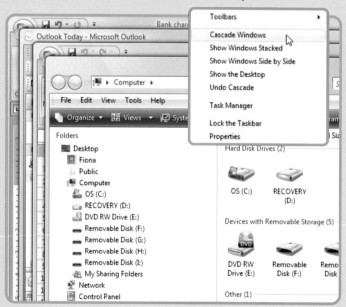

3 If you're working with two related documents in different programs, it can help to have the two windows side by side on screen. To do this, open both documents, right-click on the **Taskbar** and choose **Show**

Windows Side by Side. You can now work in either window simply by clicking anywhere in it. Note that if you choose 'Show Windows Stacked', the windows will occupy the top and bottom halves of the Desktop.

Expert advice
To switch off the live windows previews
in Windows Aero, right-click on the
Taskbar and select **Properties**. Then
click on the box marked 'Show window
previews (thumbnails)' to uncheck it.

6 Windows Aero groups together windows from the same program on a single button on the Taskbar. Click on this button to view a list of the window titles and hover the mouse pointer over an entry to see a thumbnail image. If you prefer not to have buttons grouped, right-click on the Taskbar and select **Properties**, then click on **Group similar taskbar buttons** to uncheck the box.

5 Windows Vista has a useful new feature called Windows Aero to help organise your work. When a window has been minimised to a button on the Taskbar, you can view a thumbnail preview of it by hovering your mouse pointer over the button.

Bright idea
Press Ctrl + Windows key + Tab **to keep Flip 3D open. You can then** press Tab **(without holding down any other key) to cycle through the windows.**

Close up
In Flip 3D, one of the icons or previews displayed will be for the Desktop itself, giving you a quick way to show the Desktop and minimise the other Windows.

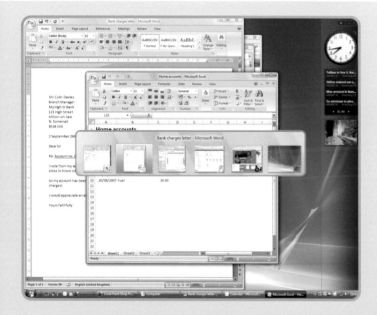

8 Windows Flip 3D offers another visually dramatic way to switch between windows. Press and hold down the **Windows key** and then press **Tab**. Your open windows are now displayed in a 3D stack. Press the **Tab** key repeatedly, or rotate the mouse wheel to cycle through the windows. Release the Windows key to display the window at the front of the stack.

7 Windows Vista allows you to switch between open windows using its new 'Windows Flip' feature. Press and hold down the **Alt** key, then press the **Tab** key. Your open windows are now displayed in a bar running from left to right across the middle of the screen. With the **Alt** key held down, press the **Tab** key until the window you want is highlighted, and then release it.

File your work

Your hard disk is like a virtual filing cabinet: each document is stored in a folder, as are all the programs you use. Also, folders can be stored in other folders, like drawers in a cabinet. It's tempting to keep all your documents on your Windows Desktop where you can see them but, as with a real desk, life is much easier if you avoid clutter and confusion.

SEE ALSO...
- *What is Windows?* p12
- *Using Windows Explorer* p24
- *Deleting files* p34
- *Maintain your hard disk* p80

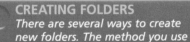

CREATING FOLDERS
There are several ways to create new folders. The method you use depends on how and where you save your work. Here are three ways to make a new folder.

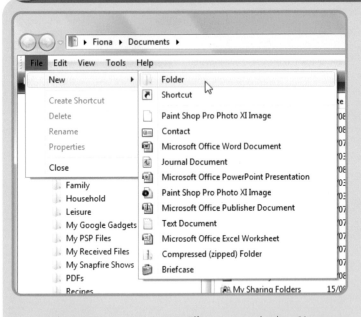

1 Always create new folders for your work within the Documents folder, or in a folder inside Documents. First, click on the **Start** button and choose **Documents**. Then click on the **File** menu and select **New** then **Folder**. It's also possible to add a new folder inside an existing folder. To do this, find the folder within Documents and double-click on it before creating your new one.

2 Your new folder will appear in the right-hand pane. The highlighted name, 'New Folder', is the default name and will be replaced as soon as you begin typing in your preferred folder name. Choose a recognisable and memorable name for your new folder and then press **Return**.

Finding lost files

If you can't find a file or folder, click on the **Start** button, then on **Search**. Type the file name, or as much of it as you can remember, in the 'Search' box at the top right. As you start typing, matching files and folders are displayed in the right pane below. Hover your mouse pointer over a match for more detail.

Expert advice

Always name your files logically so that, if you forget a file's full name, you can still perform a search for it. If several family members use your PC, and you haven't set up 'User Accounts' (see page 44), you can still create folders for each person. Use names or initials when naming documents to distinguish one person's files from another.

3 You can also create a new folder within the Documents folder while you are saving. Open a document, click on **File** and choose **Save As**. In the Save As dialogue box click on the **New Folder** button. In the New Folder dialogue box give the folder a name, then click on **OK**. Double-click on your new folder and then click on the **Save** button to store your document inside the folder.

4 Alternatively, you can create new folders in any folder window by using your right mouse button. Open the folder in which you want to create your new folder. Then right-click on a blank area, select **New** and choose **Folder**. The default name on the folder that appears will be replaced as you type in the new name.

Copy and move files

There are many reasons why you may need to copy or move a file or folder – you may want to make a backup of an important document, or perhaps you need to copy files to a CD or DVD so you can transfer them to another PC. Maybe you just want to move a file to another folder on your hard disk. Whatever you want to do, Windows makes it easy.

SEE ALSO...
- *Using Windows Explorer p24*
- *File your work p30*

BEFORE YOU START
To copy to a CD or DVD, follow the first three steps. To copy to your hard disk, open Documents, then click on the **Folders** button and follow the steps on page 33.

COPYING TO A CD OR DVD

1 Insert a disc into the drive and select **Burn files to disc** in the AutoPlay window. Give your disc a title, then click on **Show formatting options**. If you want to rewrite to the disc later, choose **Live File System**. To prevent the disk being overwritten, select **Mastered** instead. Then click on **Next**.

2 Click on the **Start** button and then on **Documents**. In the left pane, navigate to the folder or file you wish to copy. In the right pane, click on the file or folder to be copied. Keep your finger pressed on the mouse button and drag the file onto the **CD/DVD** drive icon in the left pane. When the icon is highlighted, release the mouse button.

3 A dialogue box opens to show the copying progress. If you see that you are copying the wrong file, or the right file to the wrong place, click on **Cancel**. When finished, click on **Close session** from the **File** menu and remove the disc from the drive.

Moving files

As with a conventional paper filing system, you will often want to move your files and folders. Windows helps you do this. Click on the file or folder and, keeping your finger pressed down on the left mouse button, drag it over to the new location. When the destination folder is highlighted, release the mouse button and the file or folder will move.

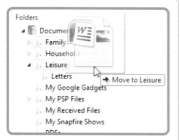

Watch out

When you drag a file from one drive to another – from your hard disk to the CD or DVD drive, for example – you are left with two identical files: one on the original drive and an exact copy on the destination drive. If you drag a file to a different place on the same drive, the file will just move, without making a copy.

MAKING COPIES OF FILES

1 To make a copy of a file that is stored on your hard disk, first open the folder that contains the file that you wish to copy. Then click on the file once to select it, click on the **Edit** menu and select **Copy**.

2 Now locate the folder into which you wish to paste a copy of the selected file. Double-click on it, then click on the **Edit** menu and select **Paste**. An exact copy of the file will appear in the right-hand pane of the window.

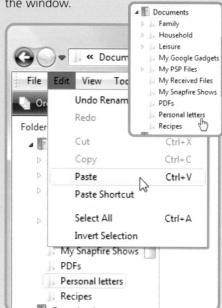

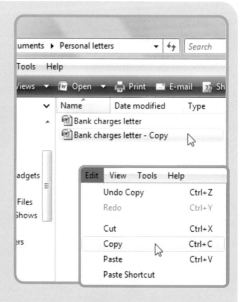

3 You can also store a copy of a file within the same folder as the original. Click on the relevant file, click on the **Edit** menu, select **Copy** and then click on **Edit** again followed by **Paste**. To distinguish the copy, Windows appends ' - Copy' to the name of your original file.

Deleting files

Regardless of how fast or powerful your computer is, it will begin to slow down if the hard disk gets too full. There will also be less disk space available for new files and programs. It's therefore a good idea to delete redundant files and folders regularly, moving them from your hard disk to the Recycle Bin. This, in turn, needs to be emptied to free up the disk space.

SEE ALSO...
● *Maximise your disk space p76*
● *Uninstall old programs p78*
● *Maintain your hard disk p80*

THROWING ITEMS AWAY

It's easy to dump unwanted files or folders in the Recycle Bin. And if you throw one away by mistake, you can retrieve it just as quickly.

Delete options

There are a number of ways to put an item in the Recycle Bin: you can drag and drop the file or folder onto the bin icon; select the file and press the

Delete key on the keyboard; or right-click on the file and choose **Delete**. When you choose to delete a file (unless you drag it to the bin), Windows will ask you if you are sure you want to do this. Click on the **Yes** button to confirm the action. Note, the bin icon will be hidden if you are in a maximised window, so you will not be able to use the drag and drop method to delete an item.

The Desktop icon shows an empty bin when there is nothing in it and displays contents in the bin when it contains files. You can view the contents of the Recycle Bin by double-clicking on it. Putting files in the bin does not free up disk space, as the files are still stored on your hard drive. In order to free up the space, you must empty the

Recycle Bin. With the Recycle Bin window open, you can see a list of its contents in the right-hand pane, with options for emptying the Bin and restoring files on the dark-coloured menu bar above. Click on **Empty the Recycle Bin** to permanently delete all the files. If you do not want to delete all the files in one go, select the ones you know that you no longer want, click on the **File** menu and choose **Delete**. You will need to confirm your action.

Restoring files

Open the Recycle Bin and select **Restore all items** from the dark-coloured menu bar. This will return the files to their original locations on your PC. If you just want to restore one file, select it and click on **Restore this item**.

Bright idea
If you want to delete a few files at the same time, select them all by clicking on the first file, holding down the Ctrl key and the clicking on the others in turn. You can then delete them collectively using the methods described above.

Watch out
Files deleted from a CD, DVD or other removable storage media will not be placed in the Recycle Bin. Also files too large for the Bin will be deleted immediately. If this is the case, Windows will display a warning box.

THE RECYCLE BIN PROPERTIES

The storage capacity of the Recycle Bin can be increased or decreased to suit your requirements – but you may need to take the size of your hard drive into consideration.

Adjusting the capacity of the bin
Right-click on the **Recycle Bin** icon, choose **Properties** and, with the **General** tab selected, you can determine just what proportion of the hard disk you are prepared to allocate to the storage of files in the Recycle Bin.

The 'Custom size' box gives the default size of your hard disk. You can increase the hard disk space by typing a higher figure into the box. If you work with lots of large files, you may want to increase the figure to 25% of its original size to allow for their storage. But you should bear in mind that if you allocate a lot of hard disk space to the Recycle Bin, you must empty it regularly or it will gradually fill up your hard disk. This may result in your PC slowing down

and eventually you will receive a warning that disk space is low. When you reach the limit of your Recycle Bin's storage capacity, your PC will automatically begin to delete the files in the bin, starting with the oldest ones.

Deliberate deletion
If you wish, you can get rid of the Confirm File Delete dialogue box that appears when you move a file or folder to the bin. In the Recycle Bin Properties dialogue box, remove the tick next to 'Display delete confirmation dialog', then click

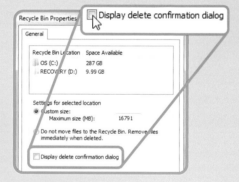

on **Apply** and **OK**. Your files or folders will now go straight into the Recycle Bin.

If you are sure that you will never need a file again, hold down the **Shift** key when you drag it into the Recycle Bin (above). The Confirm File Delete dialogue box does not appear and the file is deleted without being held in the bin.

Alternatively, you can put a tick next to 'Do not move files to the Recycle Bin. Remove files immediately when deleted' in the Recycle Bin Properties box. Only use these methods if you are confident that you no longer need your documents because, once you have done this, the files can only be recovered with the help of specialist software, such as Norton Utilities.

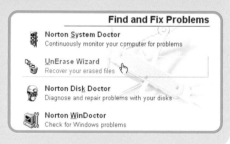

That's amazing!
Even the most basic computers now come with 80–160GB hard disks – on more expensive models they can be as much as 320GB or 500GB. Even these huge capacities can be filled with large amounts of photos or music files, however. It is therefore good practice to delete old files on a regular basis.

Finding files

Once you have been using your computer for a while you may build up a large collection of files and programs. Even with an efficient filing system, it is possible you may not be able to find a document that you need. Windows Vista's Search facility not only allows you to locate files on your PC, but also enables you to find Web sites and information via the Internet.

SEE ALSO...
- *Using Windows Explorer p24*
- *File your work p30*

THE SEARCH IS ON

Regardless of how many files are stored on your PC, Windows can locate any one of them quickly – even if you're not sure of the file name.

Locating files

If you are having trouble finding a specific file, the first place to look for it is in your Documents folder. If you can remember in which folder you normally save your work – for instance, 'Letters' or 'Personal Files' – then that's the first place to look.

If your file isn't there, and you know that it was worked on recently, click on the **Start** button and then on **Recent Items**. This lists the last 15 files that were opened on your computer, even if you did not make any changes to them. If the file you want is listed, click on it once to open it. If neither of these

methods proves successful, you may have accidentally saved your file in the wrong folder or dragged it to the Recycle Bin. In this case you will need to use the Windows Search tool.

Searching in the Start menu

The Start menu gives you a very easy way to locate files, folders and programs. Click on the **Start** button, then start typing a word that you

know is part of the document you want, for example, 'letter'. There is no need to click in the box. As you type, relevant files, folders and programs appear in the left-hand pane, replacing the normal display of programs. When the one you want appears, click on it to open the file in its associated program.

Close up
If you click on the Search button on any folder toolbar, it opens the Search For Files and Folders facility in the left-hand pane of the folder window.

That's amazing!
If you have forgotten a file's full name, you can use the '*' symbol (type **Shift + 8**) to search for it. When you use the asterisk in a search, it represents any character or characters in the file name. If you only know that your file name started with an 'S', type 's*', or if your file is a Word file that ends with the name 'john', type '*john.doc'.

WINDOWS' SEARCHES

Some files are easier to find than others, so try a basic search first. If that doesn't work, use the advanced search.

Basic search

All Vista windows contain a 'Search' box in the top right corner, so finding files and folders is very easy. Type your search word or words into the search bar. As you type, matches from the current folder and its sub-folders will begin to appear in the right-hand pane below. To select a file and open it, just double-click on the filename.

Type-specific search

If the basic search has not found your file, or has returned too many results to look through, try targeting your search more specifically. Click on the **Start** button and then on **Search**.

You will be presented with a new search window. In the search box at the top right, start typing as before. The search engine will now look at filenames and folders, and will search

inside files within your user area. To break the search down further, click on one of the options in the 'Show only' bar – limiting the search to documents or pictures, for example.

Advanced search

If you still cannot find your file, Vista provides an Advanced Search. After each search for files and folders, a prompt appears at the bottom of the right pane in the results window asking 'Did you find what you were searching for?'. Below this is an **Advanced Search** button. Click on this and an extra panel of options appears at the top of the window above the menu bar.

Using this panel you can specify additional search criteria to help narrow down your search. Use the drop-down menus to search by Location, Date and Size, or specify a name, tag or author of a file in the appropriate box. Fill in what you know and then click on **Search**. Your results will appear in the right-hand pane below.

Here is a short explanation of the 'Advanced Search' features:

Date – this is useful if you know roughly when the file was last saved.

Size – searches on the basis of file size, so if you are looking for a large image you can search for all files over, say, 1MB.

Name – enter the name of the file or folder you wish to find.

Tags – these are keywords you may have chosen to add when saving the file – they are very useful if you do need to search for it later.

Authors – this is the name of the originator of the document and anyone else who has modified it.

Sorting your results

When a search is complete, your results will be listed in the order in which Search located them. This is because Search looks in a specific sequence of locations. Click on the **Type** column heading above the file names to see the results grouped together by type, with folders first, followed by any relevant files. Click on the **Type** heading again to view the results in reverse alphabetical order.

Watch out
Remember that, with all searches, if you type in 'count' search will also find 'account', 'accountant' and 'accountancy'.

Windows Live Messenger

The ability to communicate electronically via the Internet is integral to Windows Vista, and Live Messenger plays a key role in providing this. With this program you can chat and instantly swap files with contacts, and even conduct video conferences or telephone calls. It's easy to set up so you'll soon be chatting on-line, anywhere, at any time.

Watch out
Never reveal your address, telephone number, bank account or credit-card details to anyone in a chat room or individual message window, even if you know the person to whom you are talking.

BEFORE YOU START
If you are not already on-line, open Help and Support (see page 90), search for 'Internet connection' and click on 'Connect to the Internet'.

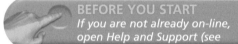

1 Go to the **Start** menu, select **All Programs**, then **Windows Live Messenger**. If you don't already have a Windows ID, click on the **Sign up for a Windows Live ID** link at the bottom, and follow the step-by-step instructions (see page 39). When you next open Windows Live Messenger, click on **Sign in** to begin chatting.

2 Once Messenger is set up, your Messenger window appears on screen. To close the window, make it larger or minimise it, use the buttons on the top right-hand corner. To open the window, double-click on the Messenger icon on the Taskbar at the bottom right of your screen.

3 To add a Messenger contact, select **Add a contact** from the Contacts menu. Enter your contact's details in the 'Instant Messaging Address' box and type an invitation message and other relevant details, then click on **Add contact**. Your contact will receive a message and, if they accept, you will be connected.

Sign up for Messenger

If you haven't used Messenger before, you will need to sign up and download the software to your PC. Follow the instructions in Step 1 and click on **Download it FREE now!**, then on **Save**. When prompted, click on **Run** and then on **Run** again to start the wizard. Follow the prompts and click on **Finish** to complete the installation.

Do not disturb

If you want to browse the Internet or send and receive e-mail but don't want to be contacted via Messenger, you can set your status as 'Appear offline'. Contacts who have you in their contact book will then see your name as 'Not online' and will not be able to initiate chats. Click on your name (see right) to set this status.

4 To send a message, double-click on your contact. A conversation window opens. Type your message in the bottom section and click on **Send**. Leave the window open and the reply appears under your message. Close the window and the reply pops up at the bottom right of your computer screen – click on it to continue your chat.

5 To initiate a three-way conversation, click on **Invite someone to this conversation**. Choose and click on a Messenger buddy in the next box, then click on **OK**. When you finish chatting, simply close the window. Messenger is still running, so you can double-click on the bottom-right icon when you want to chat to someone new.

6 With Windows Live Messenger you can share files on your PC with someone else, which can be a great alternative to sending large files by e-mail. Simply drag a file – a photo or a document, for example – onto a contact's name, and a Sharing Folder is automatically created. You can add as many files, of any file type, as you like in this manner. Now you and that person can access all the files in the folder any time, even if one of you is off-line.

Quick keyboard commands

Nearly all the actions or commands you perform with your mouse can also be done by pressing 'hot keys' – these are single keys or combinations of keys. For example, you can access the Start menu by pressing the 'Windows' key at the bottom left of your keyboard, or you can open 'Computer' by pressing the 'Windows' and 'E' keys together.

HANDY HOT KEYS

Use key commands to select menu options and navigate Windows.

Selecting main menu options
The menu bars in Windows programs all look similar and contain common menus such as File, Edit and View. On these menu bars, one letter is underlined in each menu item, for example, 'File' or 'Format'. In Windows Explorer you have to press the **Alt** key (to the left of the Spacebar on the keyboard) to see these letters.

In any window, press **Alt** followed by the underlined letter in the menu item to open the menu:

Alt + **F** to open the File menu
Alt + **E** to open the Edit menu
Alt + **V** to open the View menu
Alt + **A** to open the Favorites menu
Alt + **T** to open the Tools menu
Alt + **H** to open the Help menu.

Using the Function keys
The Function keys, also known as the 'F keys', at the top of the keyboard perform preset actions. For example, press **F1** to access a program's Help database. From the Windows Desktop, press **F3** to access the Search Results dialogue box. You can also use Function keys in combination with other keys. To close a window or program, for example, press the **Alt** and **F4** keys together.

Moving around the Desktop
You can use keyboard shortcuts to move around your Desktop. For example, click anywhere on the Desktop, then press the arrow keys to move to any icon (they are highlighted when selected). Press the **Return** key to open the selected item.

The same principle can be applied inside folders. Open the Documents folder then press the arrow keys to move around the folder's contents. Press **Return** when you want to open a selected file or folder.

Important command keys

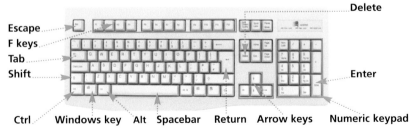

Escape
F keys
Tab
Shift

Delete

Enter

Ctrl   Windows key   Alt   Spacebar   Return   Arrow keys   Numeric keypad

Close up
If several programs are open, use the Alt and Tab keys to select one. Hold down Alt and then press Tab and a bar shows the program icons – the active one is outlined. Move through the icons by pressing Tab, and release Alt to make the outlined program active. See page 29 for more details.

Customising Windows

Personalise your Desktop

The Windows Desktop is part of your working environment and so it is important you like its appearance and colour scheme. Fortunately, you can change the background image on the Windows Desktop and the colour of the window frames with just a few clicks. You can also choose from a range of animated screensavers for when you're not using your PC.

SEE ALSO...
- *Change your settings p44*
- *Create your own shortcuts p50*

DESKTOP MAKEOVER
Windows comes with an extensive selection of Desktop backgrounds.

Background images
To change your Desktop background, right-click anywhere on your Desktop and select **Personalize** from the pop-up menu. In the window that appears, click on the **Desktop Background** link. With 'Windows Wallpapers' selected in the 'Picture Location' options, scroll through the list of available images. Click on one that interests you and your Desktop will automatically change to that image. If the image doesn't fill your screen or you would prefer it to display differently, click on one of the options beneath the pictures. Select **Stretch** (on the left) to force the image to fit the screen,

Tile (in the middle) to repeat the image over your Desktop or **Center** (on the right) to position the image in the centre of the Desktop. When you have made your choice, click on **OK**.

USING YOUR OWN PICTURES
You can use your own digital photographs, stored on the hard disk, as your Desktop background.

A truly personal Desktop
Make sure you store any pictures you have downloaded, scanned or taken using a digital camera in your Pictures folder – you can find this inside your Documents folder. Your pictures will then be available for easy selection from the 'Pictures' option, as they will appear in the 'Picture Location' drop-down list.

If you want to use pictures which are stored in another folder, click on the **Browse** button. Locate the folder containing your photograph, click on it to select it, and then click on **Open**. The image will now be displayed. Select a positioning option as previously described and click on **OK** to confirm your choice.

Bright idea
Remind yourself of an important message using a screen saver. In the Personalization window, click on the Screen Saver *link, choose the* 3D Text *screen saver and click on the* Settings *button. Then type your reminder, and select a font, colour and style. Choose how fast it scrolls across your screen, then click on* OK *and* OK *again.*

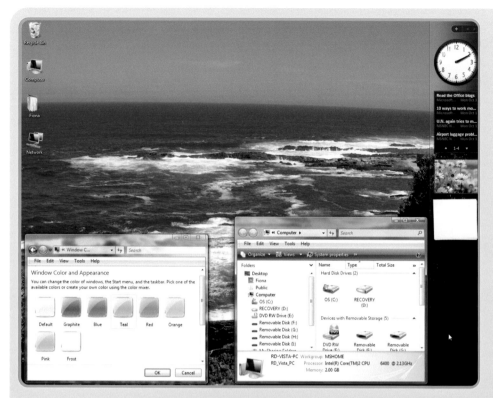

MOVING PICTURES

Screen savers are animations that appear when your PC is idle. They can also protect work from prying eyes.

Small-screen animation

To select a screen saver, right-click anywhere on the **Desktop** and select **Personalize** from the pop-up menu. Click on the **Screen Saver** link and then click on the down arrow to the right of the box under 'Screen saver'. Scroll through the list and select an option. Click on **Preview**

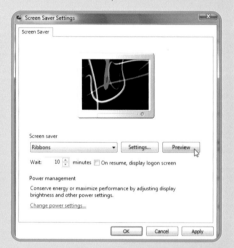

to view your choice on screen. To return to the Screen Saver Settings dialogue box, just move your mouse a little. You can now set the length of time your PC waits before activating the screen saver in the 'Wait' box. Finally, click on **OK** to confirm your choices.

COLOUR SCHEMES

Windows lets you choose different colour schemes for your Desktop.

More than just a Desktop

Open the Personalization window and click on the **Window Color and Appearance** link. Here you can choose from eight preset Windows colours, including the default.

Click on the 'Enable transparency' option to give your windows a 'glass-like' appearance. You can also click and drag on the 'Color intensity' slider to vary the depth of colour.

Save your energy

On some PCs, the Screen Saver Settings dialogue box has a power management option that reduces the amount of power used by your monitor and/or hard disk after a set period of inactivity. Click on the **Change power settings** link and the Power Options dialogue box opens. Here you can select a power plan or change its settings. To make a change, click on the **Change plan settings** link, and select the time to 'Turn off the display' and 'Put the computer to sleep' from the drop-down lists.

Change your settings

Whether it's just for fun or to make using your PC more comfortable, you can adjust many of Windows' settings to suit your needs. It's possible to alter the speed at which the mouse pointer moves and how fast you must double-click to launch an item. You can also set a series of sounds that are triggered in response to your actions.

SEE ALSO...
- *Personalise your Desktop p42*
- *User Accounts p46*

USEFUL SETTINGS

By customising a few settings you can make sure that your PC works just the way you want it to.

Mouse settings

To customise your mouse settings, click on the **Start** button and then on **Control Panel**.

Hardware and Sound
Play CDs or other media automatically
Printer
Mouse

Under 'Hardware and Sound', click on the **Mouse** link. See the 'Close up' tip below if your Control Panel shows different options.

There are five tabs at the top of the Mouse Properties dialogue box:

Buttons allows left-handed users to swap the function of the mouse buttons from left to right. You can also adjust the speed at which you need to double-click under 'Double-click speed'. To test the setting, double-click on the folder – if it opens and closes, the speed is right for you. If not, drag the slider towards 'Slow'.
Pointers lets you change your mouse pointers – double-click the pointer you want to change,

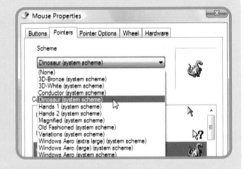

choose from the range displayed and click on the **Open** button. Alternatively, you can change all the pointers using one of the schemes in the drop-down list under 'Scheme'.
Pointer Options enables you to alter the speed at which the pointer moves in relation to the movement of the mouse, and choose whether you want the pointer to automatically snap to buttons ready for you to click. You can also

Close up
Depending on how your PC is set up, the Control Panel window may be displayed as shown above (the default), or in 'Classic view' (as with previous Windows versions). Click on Control Panel Home if your Control Panel looks different from the pictures above.

Watch out
If your PC came with a non-standard mouse, or you have upgraded your mouse, the dialogue box for Mouse Properties may look slightly different to the one shown here. However, all the features will be present, and there may even be some advanced settings for the extra mouse buttons.

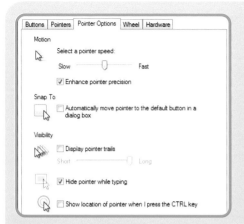

decide whether the mouse leaves a **cursor trail** or is hidden while you type.

Wheel lets you change the vertical and horizontal scrolling settings that apply when using the mouse wheel.

Hardware allows you to check whether your mouse has the right drivers installed, and if it is working properly.

Date and time

The current time is displayed on the right-hand side of the Taskbar. To see the date, hover your mouse pointer over the time display. To set the date or time, right-click on the time display. Click on the **Change date and time** button and then, in the next window, click on the hour, minutes or seconds and then on the up or down arrows to adjust each setting.

To set the time zone for your location, click on the **Change time zone** button and then on the down arrow to the right of the 'Time Zone' panel. Scroll down the list and click on the correct time zone.

Windows can also be set so that it switches between British Summer Time and Greenwich Mean Time automatically on the correct dates. To be reminded of this, click on 'Remind me one week before this change occurs'. Next, click on **Apply** and then on **OK**.

Setting sounds

You can configure Windows to play sounds to accompany a particular event. Click on the **Start** button, select **Control Panel** and click on the **Hardware and Sound** link. Under 'Sound', click on **Change system sounds**. Select the **Sound** tab and choose an event from the 'Program' list. Click on the down arrow on the right of the 'Sounds' box and make a selection. To hear a sound, click on the **Test** button beside the 'Sound' box. Click on **OK** to finish.

If you wish, you can load one of Windows' preset sound schemes. Click on the down arrow on the right of the 'Sound Scheme' box and choose a scheme. To adjust the volume, click on **Adjust system volume** under 'Sound' in the Control Panel and move the slider.

Key word
A cursor trail is a series of 'ghost' images left by your mouse pointer when you move it around the screen. It is designed to make the pointer easier to see on certain types of monitor.

That's amazing!
Your PC clock is built into the motherboard and runs even when your PC is turned off. Windows Vista makes sure your computer's clock is always accurate by checking its time against a computer on the Internet. If there's a difference, Windows updates your PC's clock.

User Accounts

Windows Vista is designed to make sharing your computer easy and secure. If several family members want to use the same PC, you can set up individual 'User Accounts' to allow each person to customise their Desktop and have their own list of favourite Internet sites. You should password-protect each account so only the correct user can access it.

SEE ALSO...
● *Personalise your Desktop p42*

NEW USERS

Creating User Accounts in Windows Vista is easy – you can decide whether a user can install and remove programs or simply access their files.

You must be logged in as an administrator (an account with full access rights) to set up a new user. Click on the **Start** button, select **Control Panel** and click on **Add or remove user accounts** under 'User Accounts and Family Safety'. (If your Control Panel looks different to the picture below, see the 'Close up' tip on page 44 to change the view.) Now click on the **Create a new account** link.

Under 'Name the account and choose an account type', type a name for your new user

and click on an account type. You can choose from 'Standard user', with access only to certain applications, files and settings, or 'Administrator' with full access rights. Next click on the **Create**

Account button to open the 'Manage Accounts' window. Click on your new user account to customise or make changes to it. You can

choose to change the account name, create a password, add a picture, set up parental controls, change the account type or delete it. If you change your mind, you can alter these settings later. Remember, you should always password protect 'Administrator' accounts.

Close up
If you want to control your children's access to sexually explicit or violent material on Web sites, you can set up Internet preferences for them. *Open* Control Panel*, go to* Network and Internet *and select* Internet Options*. Select the* Content *tab and click on the* Enable *button under 'Content Advisor' to set the ratings.*

Watch out
If you are the only computer administrator and you forget your password you will no longer be able to access many of Windows' features. To avoid this problem, create a 'password reset disk'. Open the Control Panel, click on **User Accounts** and select your account name. Then click on **Create a password reset disk** under 'Tasks' in the left-hand panel and follow the steps in the wizard.

MANAGING ACCOUNTS

Each user can have an individual picture and choose a password so no one else can access their files.

If you want to change the image Windows has allocated to your account, click on the **Change your account picture** link in the User Accounts window. Then either choose a new image from the default list of images, or browse your hard disk for one of your own pictures.

To password-protect a user's account, first click on the account you want to change and then click on the **Create a password** link. At the next screen you must enter the password twice, to confirm you have spelt it correctly. Add a password hint, then click on **Create password**.

FAST USER SWITCHING

If you regularly need to swap users, you can use Fast User Switching to allow people to log on and off while leaving their programs running.

Click on the **Start** button and hover your mouse pointer over the right-pointing arrow next to the padlock icon. From the pop-up

menu select **Switch User**. Windows will store the state of all your programs and windows and allow another user to log on. The new user will see the default Desktop image where they can click on their own user icon and type in their password. When the second user is finished, they can again choose **Switch User** from the **Start** menu and all of their programs and documents will be retained, just as with the first user. Alternatively, any user can click on **Log Off** if they have finished working for the day. If the original user wishes to return, they can just click on their icon and enter a password to restore their Desktop.

Users should always choose the 'Log Off' button if they do not intend coming back to work at the PC. Signing out of a user account will free up the memory required to store the user's Desktop and open programs.

PASSWORD CHANGES

You can, and should, change your Windows user frequently to avoid an unnecessary breach of security.

You should make sure you have a 'strong' password for your user account. A strong password is at least 8 characters long, containing no real names and is not a complete word. Use both upper and lower-case letters

plus numbers and symbols. To change your password, click on the **Start** button, **Control Panel** and **User Accounts and Family Safety**. Then click on **User Accounts** and **Change your password**. Fill in the boxes as prompted, not forgetting to enter a 'password hint', and click on **Change password** to finish.

Key word
If you have to log on to a computer to use it, you need to prove you are authorised to do so – usually by clicking on a user icon and typing a password. When you log off, you're telling the computer that you intend to stop using it for the time being.

Watch out
You can make your password as convoluted as you like, but make sure your password hint reflects this. After a long holiday, for example, you may have forgotten a complex password.

Accessibility programs

If you have a sight, hearing or mobility impairment, Windows has lots of options to make operating your PC easier. It's possible to use your keyboard to operate the mouse pointer and buttons, and you can instruct Windows to replace warning sounds with on-screen displays. You can also use an on-screen keyboard and even have Windows read out text or magnify it.

ACCESSIBILITY PROGRAMS

You can access these tools by clicking on the Start button, All Programs, Accessories and Ease of Access.

Magnify your screen
The Magnifier program is designed to help people with impaired vision. When you run Magnifier, the top section of your screen

becomes an enlarged view of your working area. It tracks what you're doing by displaying the mouse pointer or any text you're typing.

To launch Magnifier, click on **Ease of Access** and then on **Magnifier**. To make changes to the settings, click on 'Magnifier' on the Taskbar. You can choose the level of magnification, the position of the magnified area and change the screen colours, if this helps.

Use an on-screen keyboard
If you find the mouse easier to operate than the keyboard, try using the on-screen keyboard option instead. Click on **Ease of Access** and

choose **On-Screen Keyboard**. To type, click on the keys you require with your mouse. You can customise the keyboard layout and the way the keyboard works through the Keyboard and Settings menus.

Need help getting set-up?
The Ease of Access Center holds a variety of tools to help users with special needs get the most from their computers. Click on the link **Get recommendations to make your computer easier to use** to launch a wizard with five

options: eyesight, dexterity, hearing, speech and reasoning. Make the selections you need at each step and click **Next** to move to the next option – it is not essential to make a selection to go to the next step. Click on **Done** to finish.

Expert advice
To move the cursor using Mouse Keys use the numeric keypad on your keyboard: up = **8**, down = **2**, left = **4**, and right = **6**. To move diagonally, press either the **7**, **9**, **1** or **3** keys. To click, press **5**. To double-click, press the **+** (plus) key. To right-click press the **-** (minus) key followed by **5**. The '5' key will continue to act as a right-click until you press **/** to switch back to normal clicking.

Close up
If you need to make the magnified area bigger, place your cursor on the line between the normal screen and the magnified section. When the double-headed arrow appears, just click and drag to increase the area.

SIGHT, SOUND AND TOUCH

Set up your keyboard and display to suit you, making your PC as comfortable as possible to use.

Adjust your keyboard

If you find typing difficult, Windows has settings to make the keyboard easier to use. Click on the **Start** menu and select **Control Panel**. Click on the **Ease of Access** icon and then on **Change how your keyboard works**. This opens the 'Make the keyboard easier to use' box, where there are several options available. If you have difficulty holding down the Shift, Ctrl or Alt keys along with another key when you carry out a keyboard command, click to place a tick next to 'Turn on Sticky

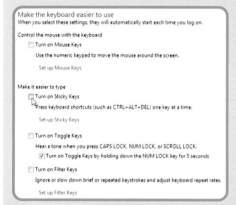

Keys'. Now click on the **Set up Sticky Keys** link below this and, in the 'Options' section, place a tick next to 'Lock modifier keys when pressed twice in a row'. Next time you want to use a keyboard command, press the **Ctrl**, **Shift** or **Alt** key twice instead of holding them down. The next option is 'Turn on Toggle Keys'. This plays a sound whenever you press the Caps Lock, Num Lock or Scroll Lock keys, so you won't leave them on by accident. If you tend to press keys more than once accidentally, put a tick next to 'Turn on Filter Keys' – Windows will then ignore brief repeated keystrokes.

Visual alerts

Select the **Replace sounds with visual cues** link in the Ease of Access Center. From here, you can switch on 'Sound Sentry', which will give a visual warning whenever your system makes an alert sound. Click on an option under 'Choose visual warning' to select the signal you get, such as 'Flash active window'. If you would like to see a caption when your PC makes a sound, tick the 'Turn on text captions for spoken dialog' option, instead of Sound Sentry.

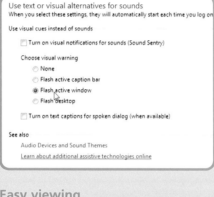

Easy viewing

If you have poor eyesight, you can make the screen easier to read. Click on the **Optimize visual display** link in the Ease of Access Center. If you click on 'Choose a High Contrast color scheme', scroll through and select from the list of options. Under the heading 'Make things on the screen easier to see', you can set the thickness of your cursor, for example.

Keyboard mouse control

If you find the keyboard easier to use than the mouse, try Mouse Keys. In the Ease of Access Center, click on **Change how your mouse works** and then click on 'Turn on Mouse Keys'. You can now use the numeric keypad to control the movement of your mouse pointer and its button actions. To swap between using the keys as numbers and as Mouse Keys, simply press the **Num Lock** key.

Narrator

If you have a visual impairment, Narrator can help by reading out the contents of the active window, text you have typed or menu options. You can launch Narrator from the Ease of Access Center – it will appear as a button on

the Taskbar. Click on the Taskbar button to see the options. Narrator can read out any new windows and menus as soon as they are displayed and even read out text and numbers as you type them in. Hold down the **Ctrl** and **Shift** keys and press the **Spacebar** to have Narrator repeat any text. To start Narrator quickly, you can hold down the **Windows** key and press **U**, then click on **Start Narrator**.

Quick access to common tools

You can configure 'Ease of access' programs to start automatically when you log in to Windows or when you press the 'Windows' and 'U' keys. Open the Ease of Access Center, select the utility you want to configure and put ticks next to the actions to be performed. Click on **Save**.

Create your own shortcuts

Once you have an understanding of Windows and its programs, you can create 'shortcuts' to help you work more quickly. A shortcut is an icon on your Desktop or Taskbar, or an entry on your Start menu, that is linked to a program, file or folder. The shortcut launches the related item immediately, which saves you searching through multiple menus or folders.

QUICK LINKS
Create shortcuts to folders, documents and programs for quick and easy access.

Extra programs in the Start menu
You can add a program to the top of the Start menu simply by dragging the program icon onto it from its location under All Programs. Locate the item to which you want to add a shortcut, click on it and hold down the left button while you drag it to a new position above the grey line in the Start menu. Let go and the shortcut will appear.

Program shortcuts on your Desktop
To make a shortcut to a program, right-click anywhere on the **Desktop**, select **New** and click on **Shortcut**.
In the Create Shortcut window that appears, click on the **Browse** button.

Locate the relevant program in the Browse for Files or Folders dialogue box by clicking on the folders and drives under 'Select the target of the shortcut below'. Scroll down and click on relevant folders to open them. Select the program, click on **OK** and click on the **Next** button. Choose a name and click on the **Finish** button. The shortcut, which looks like the program icon with a small arrow, appears on your Desktop.

Desktop documents
You can also create Desktop shortcuts for documents that you use regularly. Locate the file in its folder and right-click on it. Click on **Send To** on the pop-up menu and then choose **Desktop (create shortcut)**. A shortcut icon appears on the Desktop. Drag and drop the shortcut wherever you like on the Desktop.

An alternative method is to drag the item to your **Desktop** while holding down the right mouse button instead of the left button. When you let go, a pop-up menu appears. Choose **Create Shortcuts Here** to put the shortcut on your Desktop. Now, to open the document, just double-click on the shortcut icon.

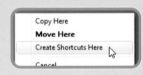

The ultimate time-saver
Set up a program to launch when you start your PC. Click on the **Start** button and choose **Computer**. In the right-hand pane, find the program on the hard disk. Drag the program over your **Start** button without letting go. Hover the mouse there and the Start menu will open. Now hover the icon over **All Programs** and, when its submenu opens, drag the icon to **Startup** and then to its submenu. Now release the mouse button. This 'drops' the program and puts a shortcut into the Startup folder.

Close up
To remove a program shortcut, click on it and drag it onto the Recycle Bin. This won't delete the program itself, which is still in the Program Files folder, because the shortcut is just a link to it.

Windows' Built-in Programs

Using WordPad and Notepad

Windows comes with a basic word processor called WordPad. Despite its simplicity, this program can be used to create documents containing a mixture of formats and graphics. Windows also includes Notepad. This is a very simple text editor, which is useful for creating documents such as Web pages, where hidden text formatting codes might cause problems.

Key word
A font is a specific style and set of characters within a typeface, for example 'Arial Bold Italic' or 'Times New Roman'.

BEFORE YOU START
Click on the Start button and select All Programs. Then click on Accessories and scroll down to WordPad and click to open it. A blank document will appear.

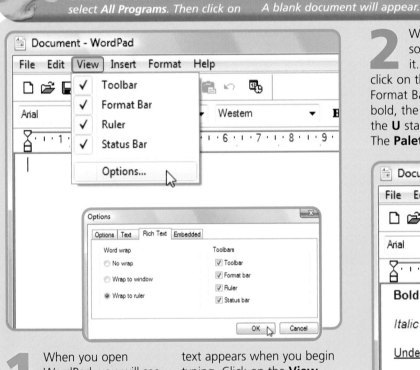

1 When you open WordPad, you will see a blank page with a flashing cursor at the top. This is called the 'insertion point' – the place on screen where the text appears when you begin typing. Click on the **View** menu, choose **Options** and click on the **Rich Text** tab. Then put a dot next to 'Wrap to ruler' and click on **OK**.

2 When you've typed in some text, try styling it. Select the text and click on the buttons on the Format Bar: the **B** stands for bold, the **I** stands for italic, the **U** stands for underline. The **Palette** enables you to choose a text colour. Next to these are the alignment buttons. You can choose to align your text to the left, the centre or the right. Click on the **Format** menu to see more styling options.

52

Bright idea
To select a word, click just before or just after it and hold down your left mouse button while dragging across it. Quicker still, just double-click on top of the word you want to select. Clicking three times in quick succession in WordPad highlights the whole paragraph.

Notepad

Launch Notepad by clicking on the **Start** button, followed by **All Programs**, **Accessories** and then **Notepad**. To change the font and text size, click on the **Format** menu and choose **Font** – Notepad will retain these settings until you change them again. Select **Word Wrap** to fit the text into the width of the window. If you want to apply formatting – such as colours or underline – you cannot do this in Notepad, so copy your text into WordPad. Select all the text, click on the **Edit** menu and choose **Copy**. Then open **WordPad**, click on its **Edit** menu and select **Paste**.

4 To save your page, click on the **File** menu then on **Save**. Choose a location for your file by clicking through the folders listed. Then type a name in the 'File name' box. Choose a file format in the 'Save as type' panel: to keep the formatting you have applied, choose **Rich Text Format** (Word can open rich text documents). For a plain text file with no formatting, choose **Text document**. Finally, click on **Save**. To print your page, click on the **File** menu and select **Print**. Then click **Print**.

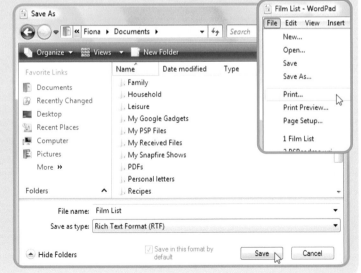

3 Now type a list, pressing the **Return** key after each item. Highlight the list and click on the **Bullets** button, or choose **Bullet Style** from the **Format** menu. To change **font**, select the text, click on the arrow next to the font name and scroll through the drop-down list to select another font. You can also change the font size in the drop-down menu to the right of the font list.

Windows Contacts

Create a comprehensive directory of everyone you know with Windows Contacts – a really useful component of Windows Mail that can hold names, addresses and other pieces of information such as birthdays. You can access your Contacts directly, or through Windows Mail (included with Windows Vista).

Watch out
If you have contact details stored in Microsoft Outlook, you will first need to export them as a separate document from Outlook into your Documents folder, and you can then import them from there into your Contacts.

BEFORE YOU START
Make sure all your contacts details are up to date. To open *Windows Contacts, go to the* *Start menu, All Programs, then* *Windows Mail.*

1 In the window that opens, your user name will appear under 'Folders' in the left-hand pane. Beneath your user name, click once on **Contacts** and all your contacts and contact group will display in the first column of the middle pane.

2 To create a new entry, click on the **File** menu, select **New** and then **Contact**. Under the 'Name and E-mail' tab, enter your new contact's first and last names. Next, fill in the 'E-mail' panel and click on **Add**. You can store more than one e-mail address. Select the address your contact uses most often and click on **Set Preferred**.

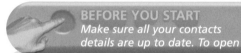

3 There are various other tabs to the right of the 'Name and E-mail' tab. Use these to add details to your contact information, such as home address, work address and family. When you've finished, click **OK**. You can create separate folders for work contacts, relatives and so on. Click on the **File** menu, select **New** and then **Folder**. Name the folder and click **OK**. To reorganise your contacts, click and drag them into the correct folder.

Bright idea
To send an e-mail to a contact in your Contacts list, right-click on their name, select *Action and then* Send E-mail*. A New Message window will open in your e-mail program with the contact's e-mail address already in the 'To' panel.*

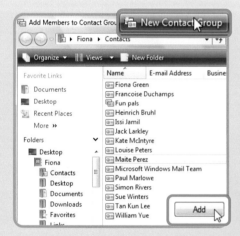

4 If you often send e-mails to several people at once – members of a club, for instance – you can collect their addresses into a 'group'. To create a new group, click on the **New Contact Group** button on the menu bar. Give your new group a name and then click on **Add to Contact Group**. Select each person, then click on **Add**. Every time you wish to e-mail those people, just type the group name in the 'To' panel of your e-mail message.

5 As your list of contacts grows, you will need a way to find the one you want quickly and easily. Click on the **View** menu and select either **Sort By**, **Group By** or **Stack By** and then select your criteria – **Name**, for example.

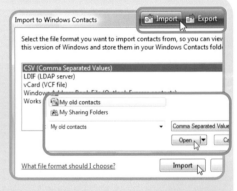

6 If you have contacts lists stored in other programs, you can import them into Windows Contacts. To do this, click on the **Import** button, select the e-mail program you wish to import from and then click on **Import**. Navigate to your saved file of contacts and click on **Open** and then on **Next**. These contacts will now be available within your Windows Contacts.

Equally, you can export your Contacts to another e-mail program. Just click on **Export** and work through the dialogue boxes to create your export file and send it to the correct destination.

Movie Maker

The latest video camera technology lets you record your movies digitally and then transfer them directly to your PC. Using the Movie Maker program supplied with Windows, you can edit those movies and then share them by saving them onto a recordable CD/DVD, posting them on your Web site, or by sending them anywhere in the world by e-mail.

Close up
When Movie Maker creates clips, these are only references to your videos – the actual files remain in their original locations on your hard disk so make sure you don't move or delete them.

BEFORE YOU START
You may need to install software for your camcorder on your PC.

Check the manual for details on how to transfer your movie clips from the camera to your PC.

1 Click on the **Start** button and select **All Programs**, then **Windows Movie Maker**. Once you have copied your video across to your PC, click on **Import video** in the Movie Tasks pane and browse to the folder in which you stored your videos. Select a file and click on **Import**. Movie Maker converts your video to 'clips', which it places in the Collection pane. You can play a clip by selecting it and clicking on the **Play** button (see right) in the Monitor pane.

2 Along the bottom of the window is the 'Storyboard'. To insert the clips in your movie, drag them from the Collection pane and drop them into the large squares on the Storyboard, starting at the left. To preview your movie, click on the first clip on the Storyboard, then click on the **Play** button in the Monitor pane.

3 If you want to split a clip – if you want to delete a section, for example – select the clip in the Collection pane and move the playback indicator to the point at which you want to split it. Then click on the **Clip** menu and choose **Split**. Your clip now divides into two separate clips. Drag the one you want to use to the Storyboard and leave the one you don't want to use. Change the order of the clips on the Storyboard by dragging them. A vertical blue line shows the position the clip will occupy as soon as you let go of the button.

E-mailing your movie

If you want to e-mail your movie, select **E-mail** under 'Publish Movie' (see step 6). Movie Maker creates your movie – this may take a little while depending on how long it is. When it has finished, you are given the option to play the movie to check it one more time, or to save it before you send it. Click on **Attach Movie** when you are finished. Movie Maker opens your e-mail program and creates a new message with the movie attached.

Watch out

Not all PCs have the connector that a camcorder requires in order to 'talk' to your PC. Modern digital video cameras use a special high-speed link, which requires an IEEE 1394 (FireWire) port on your PC. If you need to purchase an IEEE 1394 adaptor in order to copy your movies to your PC, ensure that it is Windows Vista compatible.

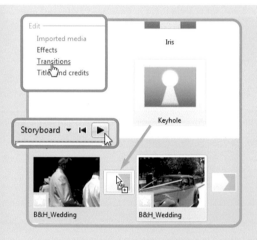

4 Movie Maker comes with built-in 'transitions'. These are animated effects that play between video clips. As one clip comes to an end, the transition takes you smoothly, using the selected effect, to the beginning of the next clip. To insert a transition, click on **Transitions** in the 'Edit' section of the Tasks pane. Click and drag a transition to the squares between the clips on the Storyboard. Click on **Back** and then on **Play** to view your changes.

5 You can add titles and credits to your movie too. Click on **Titles and credits** under 'Edit' in the Tasks pane and choose from the list of options. Type in your text – you can preview it in the Monitor pane as you type – and click on **Add Title** when you've finished. Then click on the **Back** and **Play** buttons to preview the movie.

6 Once you have all the clips and transitions in the right order (see step 3), save your movie by choosing one of the options under 'Publish to' in the Tasks pane. This launches the Publish Movie Wizard, which provides step-by-step guidance to help you save your movie in the right format. For instance, if you choose to publish to 'This computer', all you need to do is to choose a name and location for your movie and Movie Maker does the rest.

DVD Maker

The videos and digital photos that you have taken can easily be saved to a DVD, enabling you to watch them on TV and share them with others. Windows DVD Maker takes you through a step-by-step process that makes it easy to create a professional-looking DVD. You can even customise the menus and scene selection pages to suit your own project.

1 Go to the **Start** button and click on **All Programs** then **Windows DVD Maker**. On the welcome screen that appears, click on **Choose Photos and Videos**. In the 'Add pictures and video to the DVD' screen, click on **+ Add items**, then navigate to the folder holding your video and/or picture files. Click on an item to include and then click on **Add**.

2 Continue to add items to your list, as in step 1. They will appear in the window in the order that you selected them. You can now rearrange items by clicking on them in the list to select them, then on the 'Move up' or 'Move down' arrow buttons. To remove an item, you should click on it and then click on the **Remove items** button.

3 Click in the 'Disc title' box at the bottom right of the screen and enter a title for your DVD. At the bottom left, you can see a pictorial and numerical display of the amount of time, in minutes, that your DVD will run. Once your items are assembled in the correct order, click on **Next**.

Set your DVD playback options
Click on the **Options** link at the bottom right of the 'Add pictures and video to the DVD' screen to adjust various DVD settings. Under 'Choose DVD playback settings' select how the DVD will play back. Set 'DVD aspect ratio' to 16:9 for widescreen or 4:3 for standard. Set 'Video format' to PAL for UK or NTSC for US and some other countries. By default, the video format is based on the Regional and Language setting in the Control Panel.

5 To change the 'Menu style' from the default (Full Screen), scroll down the list on the right of the screen and click to select a different style. Click on **Preview** to view your changes. If at any time you want to change a previous step, click on the 'Back' arrow at the top left of the window to return to the previous page.

4 In the 'Ready to burn disc' screen, you can customise the text for the DVD menu. Click on the **Menu text** button to change the font, font colour and style. Type a new title for the Play button, Scenes button and Notes button, if you wish. Click on **Preview** to view your changes, then on **Change Text** to save your changes.

6 Now you are ready to commit your video to a DVD disc. Insert a blank DVD disc into your drive. Click on the **Burn** button at the bottom right of the window to start the burning process. This can take quite a time, depending on the amount of video to burn. A progress bar displays while the DVD is created.

Media Player

Windows' Media Player is a multimedia program supplied with Windows that allows you to play many audio and video formats. Audio sources include CDs, Internet radio stations and sound files you've downloaded from the Internet or created from a CD. You can also watch video files from CDs and DVDs, or log on to the Internet and view news footage.

GETTING STARTED
Click on the Start button, then on All Programs, scroll through the menu, then select Windows Media Player.

Understanding Media Player
Media Player is an extremely versatile entertainment program, capable of playing back most types of audio and video file. You can

control all the playing options from the Media Player window – the buttons down the left-hand side list the main features, and the buttons along the bottom control your listening and viewing settings.

Skins
You can give Windows Media Player a new look by applying a skin. Each skin has a distinct

appearance and most also incorporate the basic player functions. To apply a skin, click on **View**, then on **Skin Chooser**. From the list in the left pane, click to preview the different skins. Make your choice and click on **Apply Skin**.

Visualizations
While you are listening to music, you can watch colourful patterns, called 'Visualizations', that respond to the type of music you are playing. Click on the **Now**

Playing button, select **Visualizations** and click on the down arrow to view a sub-menu of options. Click on an option to see it in the window (make sure you have some music playing), or click on the left and right arrows beneath the Visualization window to scroll through the choices. You must click on the **Now Playing** button when you are playing music to see a selected Visualization in action.

Close up
You can view Media Player in Full Screen mode. To do so, select this option from the View *menu, or click on the button with the diagonal arrow at the bottom right of the Visualization window.*

Mini mode
If you don't want Media Player to fill your screen, run it in Mini mode. First, right-click on an empty area of your Taskbar, choose **Toolbars** and click on **Windows Media Player**. Then click on Media Player's **Minimize** button. The Player shrinks to fill a small section of your Taskbar.

THE MEDIA PLAYER WINDOW

This window gives you all the control options you need for the various Media Player features, together with a central viewing area.

Playlist chooser

Classic menu bar

Now Playing shows you what files are currently in use, for example, which CD is playing and the duration of each track.

Library allows you to organise all your favourite music, video and picture files on your PC.

Rip lets you copy audio CD tracks to your hard disk and file them in your library.

Burn allows you to transfer music, pictures and videos from your library to a blank CD or DVD.

Sync lets you copy music, videos and pictures from your library to a portable device, such as a compatible MP3 player.

Media Guide is used to find and subscribe to music, video, radio services and other types of content from on-line stores provided by Internet content providers.

Title, track, artist and composer rolling display

Time through track

Turn shuffle on/off

Turn repeat on/off

Stop

Previous track

Play/ Pause

Next track

Mute sound

Volume adjust

View full screen

Switch to compact mode

Bright idea
When you right-click on a selected CD track in the Library, you get several useful options, which allow you to rate the track, to delete it from the playlist or to view its properties. You can also select the order in which you want the tracks to play.

Close up
Click on Skin Chooser in the View menu to select from a list of colour schemes and interface styles. If you can't find one you like, connect to the Internet and click on the More Skins button. This takes you to a Microsoft Web site where you can download featured skins.

That's amazing!

Media Player can copy tracks from a CD and save them as files on your hard drive so you can listen to them without inserting the disc. These are called **WMA** files. Insert a CD and click on the **Rip** button in the Media Player window. Deselect the tracks you don't want and click on the **Start Rip** button.

Key word

WMA stands for Windows Media Audio. WMA files are compressed files, which take up much less space than the original CD audio files. However, the sound quality is not compromised, thanks to smart technology that compresses the data before it is recorded to your hard disk.

PLAYING AN AUDIO CD

1 When you insert a music CD in your CD drive, Windows will ask you what action to take. If you want Media Player to launch every time you insert an audio CD, put a tick next to 'Always do this for audio CDs'. Then click on **Play audio CD** from the list under 'Audio CD options'.

2 Media Player will begin playing the first track on the CD. If you are connected to the Internet, it will also download an image of the album cover and all the track names automatically. You can select any track by double-clicking on its name.

3 To adjust the bass or treble settings, click on the **View** menu, choose **Enhancements** and select **Graphic Equalizer**. The sliders fine tune the bass and treble – simply click and drag each vertical slider until you get the tone you want. Alternatively, you can choose a preset equaliser setting from the list under 'Custom'.

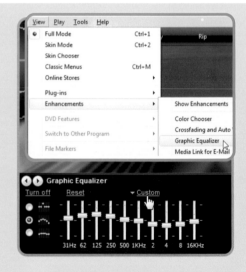

Bright idea
To adjust the volume level of Media Player, you don't need to change the overall Windows volume. Simply drag the Media Player volume slider (see page 61) to the right to increase, or to the left to decrease, the sound level.

Watch out
The sound quality of your copied audio tracks depends on the setting at which they are copied. More Kbps (kilobits per second) means the file takes up more disk space but is better quality. Less Kbps results in a smaller file but with poorer sound quality. To alter this setting, click on the **Tools** menu, select **Options**, then click on the **Rip Music** tab.

LISTEN TO ON-LINE RADIO

1 To listen to an Internet radio station, first connect to the Internet. Next, click on the **Media Guide** button on the right of the Media Player menu bar. In the panel on the right, click on **Radio Tuner** and choose from featured stations or use the preset categories to locate a station. If you know the name of a station, type it in the Search box and click on the green arrow button to the right.

2 Click on a station and a panel will open up displaying options: you can add the selected station to your My Stations list, listen to it by visiting the broadcaster's Web site or listen to it directly through Media Player. Click on the **Play** button to start listening. If a Security Warning box appears, click on the **Yes** button.

Search Results: BBC

Station Name ▲	Speed	Location
1Club.FM's Breakbeat Mix Sets (128k)	128K	Net Only
1Club.FM's Breakbeat Mix Sets (64k)	100K	Net Only
1Club.FM's Trance Channel (128k)	128K	Net Only
1Club.FM's Trance Channel (64k)	100K	Net Only
98.1 Classical KING FM (32k)	56K	Seattle, WA
BBC 6 Music (48k)	56K	Net Only
BBC Español	28K	London, Spain
BBC News (20k)	28K	London, United Kingdom

28K : News & Talk : London, United Kingdom
BBC News
▶ Add to My Station: | ▶ Play

| BBC Spanish | 28K | London, United |

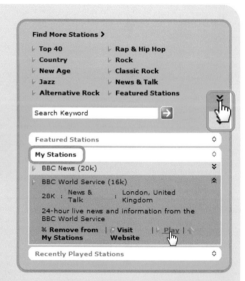

3 Use the **Back** button to return to the Radio Tuner screen at any time. From here, you can click on the **My Stations** link to see the list of stations you have added. Click on the double downward arrow button next to a station to show more information. To remove the station from the list, click on the **Remove from My Stations** link.

Close up
Windows Media Player automatically monitors your personal folders. Where it finds information about music, video or picture files, this will be added to the Library. When you play CDs, the downloaded information about the disc is also added if it hasn't already been stored.

Watch out
The Library contains links to the digital media files on your computer, but it does not hold actual copies of the files. These are contained in your Music, Videos and Pictures folders.

MEDIA LIBRARY

2 To display a different category, click on the **Select a Category** button and choose from the options displayed. To remove an entry, right-click on it and select **Delete**. A warning message will ask if you want to remove just the library link or if you want to remove the file completely. Select one option and click **OK**.

1 To display the Library, start **Media Player** and click on the **Library** button. The Library displays the category that you viewed last – in this case 'Music'. You can view the contents by Artist, Album, Songs or Genre.

Media Center

Windows Vista Home Premium edition offers a creative way of managing your digital media files. In addition, it can play CDs and DVDs, and it also supports TV and FM radio. You will need to add an FM tuner to your PC to play FM radio stations, and an analog or digital tuner is required to play and record live TV.

Expert advice
The first time you launch Windows Media Center, you will be presented with a 'Welcome' screen where you will be prompted to run the setup wizard. You will see three options: select **Express setup**.

BEFORE YOU START
To play DVDs, you must have a DVD drive and a compatible decoder. This should be pre-installed on all computers that include Windows Media Center.

1 To open Media Center, click on the **Start** button, **All Programs**, then **Windows Media Center**. You can watch your pictures in a slide show. On the blue start screen, scroll to **Pictures + Videos** and then click on **picture library**. Click on the folder of pictures (known as a 'collection') you would like to view, and then on **play slide show**. Use the toolbar to play, pause, move to the previous or next slide or end the slide show.

2 To play a DVD, insert a disc into the CD/DVD drive. If the main DVD title does not automatically display on the start screen, scroll to **TV + Movies**, and then click on **play dvd**. To skip to the next chapter on the DVD, move the mouse, and click on the **Next** button on the control bar. To go back to the previous chapter, move the mouse and click on the **Previous** button. To switch off the DVD, click on the **Stop** button.

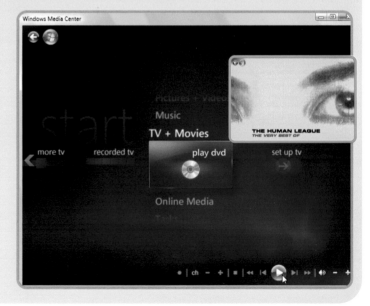

Paint

Windows' built-in Paint program is perfect for creating simple yet colourful graphics. You can use it to sketch diagrams such as maps, or to create a new pattern for your Desktop background. You might even want to design a logo or make a picture for a card. All the pictures created in Paint can be saved for use in other Windows programs.

SEE ALSO...
● *Personalise your Desktop* p42

HOW IT WORKS

Paint is perfect for making small posters, leaflets, invitations and cards.

Open Paint by clicking on the **Start** button, **All Programs**, **Accessories**, then **Paint**. The File and Edit headings on the Menu bar contain commands that allow you to open and save files, and cut and paste items as you would in a Word document. To change the size of the painting area, called the 'canvas', click on the **Image** menu and select **Attributes**.

The Tool Box

A panel on the left contains 16 tools. Hover the pointer over each to see its name.

 Free-Form Select Allows you to select an irregularly shaped area. Click and drag as if you are drawing freehand to define the selection area.

 Select Click and drag a rectangular box over an item to select it. You can then click and drag the item to move it around the canvas.

Eraser Rubs out unwanted elements of an image. Alter the eraser size using the blocks under the tool palette.

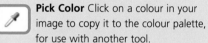 **Fill With Color** Fills a selected area with the foreground colour of your choice from the colour palette.

 **Pick Color** Click on a colour in your image to copy it to the colour palette, for use with another tool.

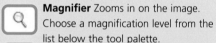 **Magnifier** Zooms in on the image. Choose a magnification level from the list below the tool palette.

Pencil Allows you to draw thin freehand lines. Click and drag to draw.

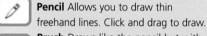 **Brush** Draws like the pencil but with 12 different style options that appear below the Tool Box.

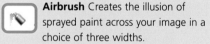 **Airbrush** Creates the illusion of sprayed paint across your image in a choice of three widths.

Text Adds words to the picture. Click where you want to begin, drag to create a text box, and type.

Expert advice
Paint can open and save 'Bitmap', 'jpeg', 'gif', 'tiff' and 'png' files. **Bitmap** is perfect for photographs saved on your PC; **jpeg** is a compressed format used for photos on Web sites and digital cameras; **gifs** can only include up to 256 colours and are used for buttons and animations on Web sites; **tiffs** are best suited to photographs; and **png** was designed to replace the 'gif' format.

Close up
If you want to reposition the Tool Box, click on any part of it that does not contain a button and drag it to another location. To return it to its original location, click and drag it to the left side of the window and it will snap back into place.

Bright idea
Hold down the Shift key while you drag out a rectangle shape to draw a perfect square. This also applies when you drag an ellipse to create a circle.

 Line Draws straight lines of the width you choose from the panel below the Tool Box.

 Curve Draws curves of a chosen width. Click to define a start point and drag to define an end point. Click on the line and drag to bend it into a curve.

 Rectangle Draw a rectangle, choosing from: an outline only, a filled rectangle with an outline, or a solid rectangle.

 Polygon Draws a many-sided figure. Click and drag for the first side, then click on subsequent points and the lines are drawn automatically.

 Ellipse Click and drag to create a circle or oval using same style options as the rectangle (above).

 Rounded rectangle This lets you draw a shape similar to a rectangle but with rounded corners.

Colours
The Color Box contains 28 coloured squares. The two overlapping squares on the left of the box indicate foreground (drawing) and background colour.

To change the drawing colour, click on a colour. To change the background, right-click on a colour.

Double-click on a colour to open the Edit Colors dialogue box. To customise the palette, click on **Define Custom Colors**. Click on a new colour in the Color Matrix and adjust the lightness with the slider on the right, then click on **Add to Custom Colors**. You can choose up to 16 custom colours to replace the preset colours. Then click on **OK**.

Saving an image
Click on the **File** menu and select **Save**. Windows saves Paint files to the Pictures folder by default. Name your file and choose a format by clicking the down arrow to the right of 'Save as type'. The best format for saving images is '24-bit Bitmap'. If you want to save space on your hard drive though, choose 'jpeg' as the file is compressed while retaining most of its quality.

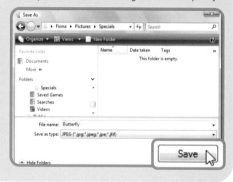

Wallpaper
You can use any image you have drawn, or one to which you have added colours or text, as the background of your Desktop. In Paint, go to the **File** menu and select **Set As Background**. Selecting the 'Tiled' option means the image will repeat across your screen (see right), while 'Centered' will position it in the middle of your screen.

Close up
To change an image on the Windows Desktop background, right-click on the Desktop and select Properties. In the Display Properties dialogue box, click on the Desktop tab and select another picture or None from the list under Background. Click on OK.

Calculator

Sometimes, when working on a document or writing an e-mail, you might need the help of a calculator. To save you scrambling through your desk drawers to find one, Windows includes an on-screen version. It works in the same way as an ordinary calculator, but you use either the numeric keypad on your keyboard or the mouse to click on the buttons.

SEE ALSO...
● *Create your own shortcuts p50*
● *Using WordPad and Notepad p52*

STANDARD CALCULATOR

To access the Calculator, click on the Start button and select All Programs, Accessories and then Calculator.

The Windows Calculator works in the same way as a normal one but some of the button symbols are different. The '/' symbol, for example, is for division and '*' for multiplication.

Numeric keypad and keyboard

All the buttons have a keyboard equivalent. The numbers and the plus, minus, multiply and divide buttons are on the numeric pad to the far right of your keyboard. Press **Return** for equals (=), **Delete** to clear the screen ('CE' in the calculator) and the **Esc** key to clear the calculation. When you use the number keypad, make sure a green light is showing next to 'Num Lock'. If not, press **Num Lock** on the keyboard to activate it.

Buttons on the left are for memory options.

M appears in this box when a number is stored in the memory.

MC clears the calculator's memory.

MR recalls a stored figure (only one can be stored at any time).

MS stores a figure in the memory.

M+ adds the figure in the display to the figure in the memory.

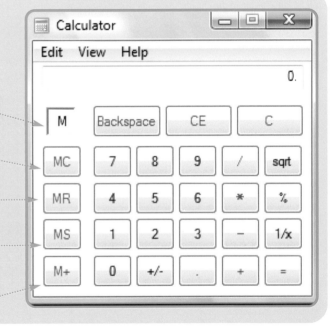

Expert advice

If you use the Calculator often, add a shortcut to the Desktop. Click on the **Start** button, select **All Programs** and **Accessories** and right-click on **Calculator**. Choose **Send To** from the pop-up list and then select **Desktop (create shortcut)**. A new shortcut appears on your Desktop – click on it and drag it to reposition it.

You can use the Standard Calculator to work out percentages. For example, to add VAT at 17.5 per cent to £150, click on the buttons to enter '150+17.5', click on the **%** button and then on the **=** button. Or you could subtract a percentage from a certain amount using the keyboard. For example, type in '£65.50-20%' and press the **Return** key.

Using the Memory

To store the displayed number, click on **MS**. To add the displayed number to the memory, click on **M+**. To see the new total, click on **MR**.

Scientific Calculator

To access a more sophisticated calculator (below), click on the **View** menu and select **Scientific**. You can work in different number base systems. We normally use decimals (Base 10), but binary, octal and hexadecimal systems (2, 8 and 16) are available. If trigonometry is your speciality, select the options at the top of the calculator for working in Degrees, Radians and Grads. There are also Inverse and Hyperbolic options. If you need to perform advanced statistical calculations, press the blue **Sta** button on the left to activate the grey buttons below it.

Digit grouping

Both the Standard and Scientific Calculators can display up to 32 digits. Add commas as thousand separators by clicking on the **View** menu and putting a tick next to 'Digit grouping'. Even with commas, the Calculator displays up to 32 digits.

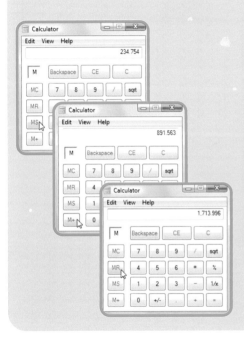

Close up
Be sure to click the C button or press the Esc key on your keyboard between each calculation. This will clear the calculator screen and ensure that your answer doesn't become cumulative.

Games

Windows Vista comes with a selection of games, ranging from the fun and easy-to-play Pinball to more challenging card games such as Hearts and the compulsive FreeCell. None of these games require special features on your PC, but an Internet connection will give you access to lots more games where you can even play against other people on-line.

EXPLORE THE GAMES

From the Start menu select All Programs, followed by Games. Then select the game you want to play.

Hearts

Click on **Hearts**, type your name in the panel and click on **OK**. Hearts is a game of simple strategy, played in rounds until one player reaches a score of 100, at which point the player with the lowest score wins the game.

At the beginning of the first round, each player chooses three cards to pass to the opponent on their left – you should pass high-scoring cards (kings, queens and aces) and high hearts, as you want to avoid winning 'tricks'. Simply click on the three you want to pass on and then click on the **Pass** (arrow) button.

On the next round, the three cards are passed to the right and on the third round,

to the player opposite. On the fourth round, no cards are passed. This continues throughout the game and Windows sets this up automatically for you. When each player has passed three cards, the player holding the two of clubs begins the first hand by playing it. Each player,

moving clockwise, must play a card of the same suit if he or she has one. Otherwise any card can be played (note that on the first trick you cannot play a heart or the queen of spades).

The trick of four cards is won by the player who plays the highest card of the same suit as the first card played.

At the end of a round, all the cards in the tricks you have won are added up – you will be allocated one point for each heart, and 13 points for the queen of spades. If a player collects all the hearts and the queen of spades, this is known as 'Shooting the Moon' – in this case, the other players each get 26 points while the player with the full hand gets none.

Remember who has scored the most points – unless you are the player with the least points, you don't really want to force the high-scoring player to go over 100 points until you are in a better position.

That's amazing!

If you are playing on a networked PC, you can have up to four people playing the same game of Hearts at the same time. And if there are only two or three of you, the computer will simulate the other players.

Bright idea

Use 'ducking' to avoid winning tricks. This is where you play the highest card you have that is lower than the highest card played by the others. Watch out though, as you could end up with high cards near the end of a round.

Solitaire

The object of Solitaire is to end up with four stacks of cards – one for each suit – at the top right of the screen in ascending suit order (beginning with the aces).

At the start of play, there are seven stacks of cards in a row – the first holds one card, the last holds seven. The top cards are face up. If any are aces, you can use the mouse to move them to the four stacks at the top right of the screen

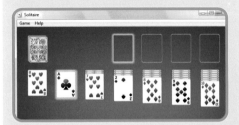

immediately. You must build the seven stacks by dragging a card to another card of the opposite colour and one higher position in the suit – for example, the jack of clubs can be placed on the queen of hearts, or the seven of diamonds can be placed on the eight of spades. You can also drag across a sequence of cards. If you can't move any cards from other stacks, click on the deck at the top left to draw new cards, and drag them to the stacks where possible.

As aces come up, double-click on them to place them on the stacks at the right. Start to build up the suit stacks by dragging the cards around. If a column is empty, you can either drag a king there from the deck or drag a

sequence of cards starting with a king from another stack. Then turn over a new card in the stack, if there's one left.

Under the 'Game' menu there are several options: **Deal** starts a new game; **Options** allows you to choose whether cards are dealt in groups of three, or one at a time; and **Deck** enables you to change the pattern of your deck by selecting one of the options.

FreeCell

Click on the **Game** menu in the FreeCell window and select **New Game**. Click on **Select Game** to choose a specific game numbered between 1 and 1,000,000. In theory, every game can be won, but you can go back to restart a game that has beaten you.

FreeCell differs from most Solitaire games because all the cards are visible right from the start. The object is similar to Solitaire, which is to get all of the cards into the Home cells at the top right of the screen, in the same suits, ascending from the ace. Move cards by clicking on them, and then clicking where you want them to go. You can only move a card to another column when it is one card lower than its destination card in rank or number and is the opposite colour – sequences of cards can also be moved. There are four cells at the top left where cards can be temporarily placed and brought back into play later. When a column is empty, you can move other cards onto it. If you are not sure what card is beneath another, right-click on the visible portion to reveal it.

Bright idea
If you want to play a game without anyone else knowing, open another program, such as Word or Excel, and use the Minimize button to reduce it to an icon on the Taskbar. While playing the game, a quick click will restore the work window, hiding your game.

Minesweeper

When the game opens you will see a pad with a grid of grey squares. A number of bombs are hidden beneath the squares. Click on the **Game** menu to choose your level – this alters the size of the grid and the number of bombs.

The timer starts when you click on your first square. Click on any square in the grid. It will either disappear, taking lots of adjoining empty squares with it and displaying numbers on those around the edges, or show a bomb and explode (meaning that you've lost the game).

Numbered squares tell you how many bombs are in the eight squares surrounding the one you have selected. Using skill and logic, you can deduce where the bombs are hidden. Right-click to put a warning flag on a square you think is hiding a bomb. Right-click twice to place an 'unsure' question mark instead.

Inkball

Use the mouse to draw ink strokes to guide the balls into holes of the same colour and to block balls from entering holes of a different colour. The game ends when a ball enters a hole of a different colour or the game timer runs out. A game also ends if you choose a different level from the **Difficulty** menu, choose **New Game** from the **Game** menu, or close Inkball. Grey is a neutral colour. Grey balls can enter a hole of any colour, and a grey hole can accept a ball of

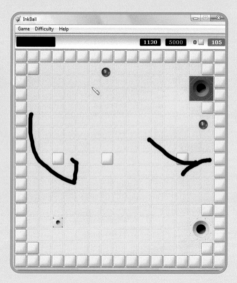

any colour, but no points are awarded. When a ball bounces off an ink stroke, a wall, or another ball, it does so at the same angle that it struck. An ink stroke disappears when a ball hits it. A single ink stroke can only affect one ball.

Spider Solitaire

If you want a better chance of winning a card game, Spider Solitaire is for you. The object is to clear the board of cards by stacking them from king to ace in the left-hand corner of the board, but this time there are ten columns. The only criteria is that the cards must be stacked in

descending order. Once the game has loaded, a Difficulty dialogue box appears on screen offering different levels. In the easiest level, all cards are the same suit, while in the most difficult level there are four suits. You can place any colour card on another one, but you cannot move a column of cards unless they are all of the same suit.

Watch out
If you want to play 3-D games, check that your PC's specifications match the game's recommended minimum requirements. These will be printed on the side of the box. The main considerations are the amount of RAM in your PC and how powerful your graphics card is.

The scoring system means that you start with 500 points and lose a point every time you move a card or undo a move. You gain 100 points for each king to ace stack you complete. Try to free up cards from the top of stacks to keep cards in suits for added flexibility. If you are stuck for a move, press **M** and the computer suggests one.

Chess Titans

Based on the conventional game of Chess, players take turns to move their pieces across

the board – one piece per turn. The first time you play, you'll be invited to select a difficulty level between one and ten, one being the easiest. Click on a piece, and the squares where you can move that piece will be displayed in blue; squares where you can capture an opponent's piece will be red. Players can't move to squares occupied by one of their own, but any one piece can capture any other of their opponent's pieces.

Mahjong Titans

To start, select the type of tile layout you want: Turtle, Dragon, Cat, Fortress, Crab or Spider. Click to select the first tile you want to remove, then click on a matching tile and both will disappear. Only exact matches will be removed,

both the class and number (or letter) must be the same. The exceptions to this are that any flower can match any other flower, and any season can match any other season. To remove two tiles, they must both be 'free' – ie, if the tile can slide free of the pile without bumping into other tiles, it is free. A pop-up note will tell you if a tile is not free.

Purble Place

Aimed at the younger generation, Purble Place is an educational and entertaining game. There are three different types of game you can play that can help teach colour, shapes and pattern recognition. As players get better, they can make the game more difficult by increasing the

complexity of tasks they have to finish or by turning on the timer to speed up play.

Other games

There are many other games that you can play, but they have to be purchased. Some are games of skill or logic, others use your PC's power to create virtual 3-D worlds, in which you can pilot a jet plane, play a round of golf on a famous course, race in a Formula 1 Grand Prix, play in a World Cup football match or seek treasure in lost tombs with explorers.

Generally, games only take up a moderate amount of disk space, but you may need to keep the game's CD in the drive while you play. Most have an auto-install feature to guide you through their setup before you first play them. The more powerful your computer and its graphics card, the faster and more realistic the games will be.

Many gaming sites on the Internet allow you to play against other people, although you may have to download an extra piece of software to do so.

That's amazing!
The Microsoft Games Center (www.zone.com) enables you to play on-line against other people of similar ability from all over the world. The Games Center will even let you send selected messages to your opponents in their language, such as 'your move' or 'bad luck'.

Keeping Windows up to date

In an ideal world, all software would be perfect and would run without any bugs or crashes. Unfortunately, this isn't always the case. Most programs have minor problems when they are released and Windows is no exception. When Microsoft finds out about a problem, they upload a 'fix', or update, to their Web site, which can be downloaded and installed automatically.

UPDATING WINDOWS
To save you the trouble of regularly checking the Microsoft Web site for new updates, Windows does it for you.

Windows Automatic Updates
Allowing Windows to download and install updates automatically keeps you up to date

without having to remember to perform an update check. Windows Update downloads just the files – or parts of files that you need – ensuring that the downloads are as small and fast moving as possible. Additionally, the system downloads and installs the most critical updates before the less important ones. When an update occurs, a message is displayed at the

right of the Taskbar. Click on the message to view which updates have been installed.

Customising Automatic Updates
Click on the **Start** button, **Control Panel**, then choose **Turn automatic updating on or off** under 'Windows Update'. There are three main options. Select the first if you want the system to automatically check and install updates on a regular basis. The second lets you choose which

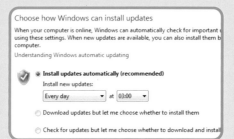

of the downloaded updates are installed. The third option allows you to decide which of the available updates are downloaded and installed.

Manually checking for updates
If you choose not to update automatically, you can still download and install the updates manually. Connect to the Internet and click on the **Start** button and **All Programs** followed by **Windows Update**. Then click on **Check for updates**. Once the scan has completed you can select the components to install.

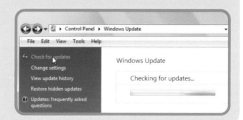

Close up
Windows Automatic Updates only downloads critical updates. If you want to check for Windows updates specific to your system, click on the Start **button,** All Programs **and choose** Windows Update. **Follow the instructions on the Web site.**

Installing updates
Some critical updates require you to restart your computer to successfully complete the installation. Always make sure that you have saved all important documents before you run Windows Update, in case you need to click on **Restart now**.

Good Housekeeping

Maximise your disk space

As you create more and more files and install new programs on your PC, your hard disk will start to fill up. If your hard disk gets too full, you will run out of room to install further programs and your PC may slow down. Keep an eye on how much space you have and regularly delete old folders and files to help keep your PC running smoothly.

SEE ALSO...
- *Deleting files p34*
- *Uninstall old programs p78*
- *Maintain your hard disk p80*

BEFORE YOU START
Look through your documents and decide which ones you need to keep and which ones to delete, if necessary. Make sure anything important is filed in a safe place.

1 To check how much space you have on your hard disk, click on the **Start** button and then select **Computer**. Under 'Hard Disk Drives' click on your hard drive icon, here **OS (C:)** and look in the bottom panel to make a quick check of how much free hard disk space you have.

2 Next, right-click on the **OS (C:)** icon and choose **Properties**. Under the 'General' tab in the Properties dialogue box, you can see the amount of used and free space in more detail, as well as your hard disk capacity. This information is given in both numerical and graphical formats. Click on **OK** to close the window.

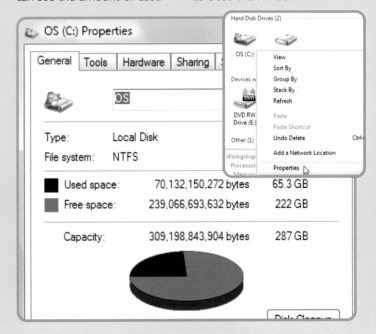

Bright idea

Remember to empty your Recycle Bin on a regular basis. It's amazing how quickly it can get filled with unwanted files and folders. This action can immediately free up a lot of disk space.

Close up

Windows Compressed Folders can reduce the size of certain files without losing any data. This process is known as compression. In any folder, right-click on an empty area, select New and then Compressed (zipped) Folder. Choose a suitable name and drag files to the folder to create compressed copies, and then delete the originals.

3 If you need to free up some space on your hard disk you have several options. The easiest option is to run 'Disk Cleanup'. Click on **Start**, **All Programs**, **Accessories**, **System Tools**, then **Disk Cleanup**. A prompt will ask if you want to clean your files only or all users' files. Make a choice, then select the drive to clean and click **OK**.

4 Disk Cleanup scans the drive to identify the files that can safely be removed. Sets of files are then listed, with the recommended deletions marked with a tick. Make changes to the selections, viewing individual files if you wish, and then click on **OK**. Deleted files won't be transferred to the Recycle Bin, so confirm you wish to permanently delete them and make the disk space available.

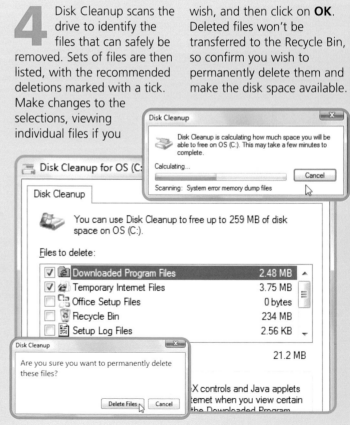

Uninstall old programs

Removing programs you no longer use frees up valuable hard disk space, but you need to uninstall them correctly. If you just put them in the Recycle Bin, problems could arise because you may not locate all the relevant files and also Windows would not know the program has been removed. You can safely uninstall most programs using the Uninstall a Program utility.

SEE ALSO...
- *Create your own shortcuts p50*
- *Maintain your hard disk p80*

BEFORE YOU START
Check that the program you intend to remove will not be wanted by other users. Go to **Start**, **Control Panel**, **Programs** and then **Uninstall a program**.

1 The Uninstall or Change a Program dialogue box will automatically open. In the right-hand panel a list of all the programs that can be removed using this process will be displayed. Scroll down the list and click on the program that you want to remove.

2 Click on the **Uninstall** button. A special uninstallation program, designed for the software you have chosen, will open. You will usually be asked to confirm your decision to uninstall. Check that you've selected the correct program and click on the **Yes** button.

Bright idea
Before you uninstall software, back up any related data you wish to keep. Ensure that you still have the original installation disks in case you want to reinstall the program at a later date.

Deleting other programs
Some programs do not register themselves with Windows and therefore don't show up in the 'Add or Remove Programs' list. If you want to uninstall one of these programs, click on the **Start** button, **All Programs** and then click on the program's folder – it should contain its own uninstallation software. Click on **Uninstall** to start the process.

3 Windows will now uninstall all the relevant program files. A dialogue box displays the progress of the operation.

If some program files are shared with other programs, you'll be asked whether you want to remove them. Just to be safe, click on **No**.

4 You may need to remove any unwanted program shortcuts on the Start menu and shortcut icons on your Desktop. Click on the **Start** menu, then **All Programs** and right-click on any shortcut or folder that belongs to an uninstalled program. Select **Delete** and click on **Yes** to confirm deletion of the shortcut. Desktop shortcuts can be dragged to the Recycle Bin.

Maintain your hard disk

To ensure that your hard disk is in optimum health, it's a good idea to perform regular maintenance. Windows has an error-checking program, which scans your hard disk and other drives for errors, and Disk Defragmenter, which reorders your data on the hard disk so that files are stored more efficiently. Both these utilities can help keep your PC running smoothly.

SEE ALSO...
- *Program crashes p97*
- *Reinstalling Windows p102*

BEFORE YOU START
It can take several hours to run Disk Defragmenter, so make sure you leave plenty of time. You can leave it to run overnight, but ensure all programs are closed.

1 To check a disk for errors, click on the **Start** button and then select **Computer**. Right-click on the drive you want to check – your hard disk should be C: – and choose **Properties** from the pop-up menu. Click on the

Tools tab and then click on the **Check Now** button under 'Error-checking'. In the Checking Disk dialogue box uncheck both 'Check disk options'. You can now perform a simple disk check by clicking on the **Start** button.

2 To perform a thorough check, put ticks next to 'Automatically fix file system errors' and 'Scan for and attempt recovery of bad sectors' in the Checking Disk dialogue box and click **Start**.

Windows cannot check a disk drive that it is currently using, so it schedules the error-checking process to take place next time you start your computer. Click on the **Schedule disk check** button to tell Windows to go ahead.

Now close all programs and restart your computer. Before Windows has finished loading, a screen is displayed giving you the option to bypass the error check by pressing any key. If you want to go ahead with the check, simply leave your PC and the error-check will start. This process may take several minutes. The progress will be displayed on screen and your computer will restart automatically when the check is complete.

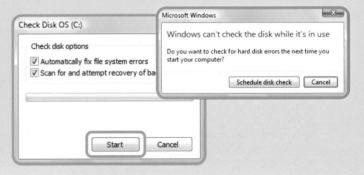

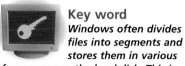

Key word
Windows often divides files into segments and stores them in various free spaces on the hard disk. This is known as fragmentation. Disk Defragmenter reorders the data.

Watch out
When you start to run Disk Defragmenter, you will be prompted for an Administrator password. Even if you are an administrator you will be asked for permission to continue.

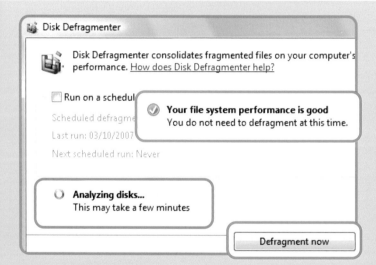

Disk Defragmenter

Disk Defragmenter consolidates fragmented files on your computer's performance. How does Disk Defragmenter help?

☐ Run on a schedul

Scheduled defragme

Last run: 03/10/2007

Next scheduled run: Never

✓ **Your file system performance is good**
You do not need to defragment at this time.

○ **Analyzing disks...**
This may take a few minutes

Defragment now

4 Alternatively, you can set Disk Defragmenter to run on a scheduled basis. To do this, click on the **Start** button, **All Programs**, **Accessories**, **System Tools**, then on **Disk Defragmenter**. Select the option **Run on a**

schedule (recommended). To change the frequency, day and time of the defragmenter schedule, click on **Modify schedule**. Select alternatives for each of the three options, by using the drop-down menus in each box.

Disk Defragmenter: Modify Schedule

⏰ **Run disk defragmenter on this schedule:**

How often:	Weekly ▼
What day:	Wednesday ▼
What time:	01:00 ▼

Disk Defragme

Disk De
perform

☑ Run on a schedule (recommended)

Run at 01:00 every Wednesday, starting 01/01/2005

Last run: 09/10/2007 14:29

Next scheduled run: 10/10/2007 01:00

✓ **Scheduled defragmentation is enabled**
Your disks will be defragmented at the scheduled time.

Modify schedule...

Defragment now

OK   C

3 You should analyse your hard disk for **fragmentation** once a month or after installing programs. To defragment your hard disk, you must be logged on as an Administrator (see page 46) and a minimum of 15 per cent free disk space is required. Go to the **Start**

menu and select **All Programs**, **Accessories**, then **System Tools**. Click on **Disk Defragmenter**. Windows then automatically analyses your disks. When completed, it reports what action, if any, needs to be undertaken. If prompted by the system, click on **Defragment now**.

Back up your work

To avoid losing important work in the event of a problem with your hard disk, it makes sense to back up your files. When you create a backup, Windows compresses your files and folders and copies them onto a storage disc. You can then update your backup files at regular intervals. This means you can restore your work if files become corrupt.

SEE ALSO...
- *Copy and move files p32*
- *Create your own shortcuts p50*
- *Reinstalling Windows p102*

BEFORE YOU START
Make sure you have adequate storage space for backing up your work. It is best to use either a recordable CD (CD-R) or DVD (DVD-R).

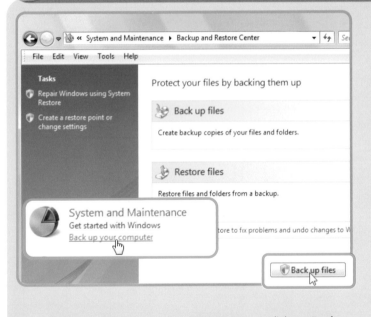

1 Windows Vista Home Premium edition includes the Windows Backup program. To start a backup, click on the **Start** button and then on **Control Panel**. Under 'System and Maintenance', click on **Back up your computer**. This will open the Backup and Restore Center. Now click on the **Back up files** button. When prompted for permission to continue, click on **Continue**.

2 Select where you want to save your backup and click on **Next**. In the next window, select the types of file that you would like to back up from the list. Note that the first backup you make will copy everything from your hard drive to the destination disc. Click on **Next**.

Expert advice
Always carefully label, date and number the discs you use for backing up. Store these discs (CDs, DVDs or external hard drive) in a secure place – a separate fireproof location is ideal.

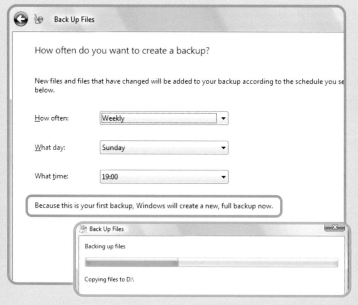

3 In the next window you can set the frequency, day of the week and time of a scheduled data backup – make your selections using the drop-down menus. However, if this is your first backup, a message will inform you that a complete backup will be performed, irrespective of the options you chose. Click on **Save settings and start backup** to begin the backup process.

4 To restore your data, launch Backup as in step 1 and click on **Restore files**. You can restore files from the latest backup or from an older set. Select an option and click on **Next**. Now, using the buttons on the right, click on **Add files** or **Add folders** and select the items to restore. If you're not sure of a file or folder name, click on **Search**, type part of the name into the box and click on **Search** to find it. When you have all the items to restore in your list, click on **Next**. Finally, select the location for your restored items and click on **Start restore**.

Power saving

Although modern PCs are designed to be as energy efficient as possible, they still use a similar amount of electricity to a television. Most PCs come with power saving options and Windows Vista has settings that let your PC economise on power if it is left idle for a certain length of time. This not only reduces your electricity bill, but helps save global energy as well.

HOW IT WORKS

You can specify exactly when you would like your computer to go into energy-saving mode.

To set Energy Saving on your computer, click on the **Start** button, select **Control Panel** and click on **System and Maintenance**. Then select **Power Options**. This opens the Power Options window.

Power plans

There are three default power plans: Balanced (gives full performance when needed and saves power when the PC is inactive); Power saver

(saves power by reducing performance, helping laptop users get the most from a single battery charge); and High performance (gives full performance, but laptop users may notice battery life is shortened).

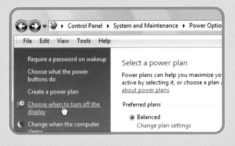

The monitor

Your monitor probably uses more electricity than any other part of your computer but it can be turned off automatically. Click on the option **Choose when to turn off the display** and

then click on the arrow next to 'Turn off the display'. Now use the drop-down menus to choose a time after which the screen will go blank (the green power light on the front of the monitor will change to orange). To restore the screen as it was before this, just move the mouse or press a key on the keyboard. Work and programs are not affected. Experiment to find your own optimum time, but remember not to make it so short that your screen turns off when you are just pausing.

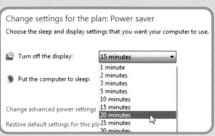

Expert advice
You can name and save different sets of power plans for use at different times, but it is likely that you will decide on one set of timings which suit you best. If you use a laptop, you can alter your current settings very quickly and easily, or even switch to another set, by using the Power Options icon on the Taskbar.

Close up
Most laptops have power-saving features. This is because they need to be portable and it is important that the battery lasts as long as possible when you are on the move.

Sleep

This allows your computer system to go into standby mode – a kind of deep sleep. It can be woken up by clicking or moving the mouse, or by pressing a key on the keyboard. Programs and windows are not closed down, so you don't have to restart or wait for Windows to start up. While this is an extremely useful option, do not use it instead of shutting down your computer when you have finished working (unless you are running a maintenance schedule). If you do and there is a power failure or your computer crashes, then unsaved work in open files will be lost. Click on the arrow beside the 'Put the computer to sleep' panel, scroll down and select a time. Or you can select 'Never', which will still enable you to set separate power saving for the monitor and the hard disk.

Advanced options

Click on the **Change advanced power settings** link to view additional options. Here you can set whether your system requires a password on wakeup. This option operates only if you have set up a user password (see page 46), and requires permission to be changed. Click on the arrow next to 'Setting' and select

'Yes' from the drop-down list, so that when you leave your machine unattended and it goes into sleep mode, a password will be requested before the PC can be used. This means no-one can access your account without your permission. The next option, 'Hard disk', sets the length of inactivity after which the hard disk will stop spinning. It is a good idea to set this to the same time as the 'Sleep' option previously described. Once you have chosen your settings, click on the **Apply** button and then on **OK** to confirm them. If you selected

the password option, a dialogue box will appear asking you to type in your password when you wake up the computer.

Restore defaults

If you find your adjusted settings unsuitable you can restore your original settings. To do this, click on the **Change plan settings** link under your plan in the Power Options window and then click on **Restore default settings for this plan**. Finally, click on **Yes**.

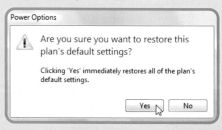

Save more energy

There are other ways of saving energy and money that you may also wish to consider. For example, you should ensure that there is sufficient space and ventilation around your computer. There is a small fan inside the system unit that cools the hard disk which needs more energy to run if there is insufficient ventilation.

Make sure hardware peripherals, such as printers, are switched off unless you are printing a document. If you schedule disk maintenance tasks (see page 80) to run during the night, leave your PC on standby – it will come to life when the task is due to begin.

Close up
Some PCs have a power feature called 'Hibernate' in which your PC saves open documents to the hard disk before going into a power-saving mode. When you restart your PC, your Desktop is restored exactly as you left it. This is useful if you are leaving your PC for an extended period.

Computer viruses

Vista is much more secure than previous versions of Windows and it is therefore less likely that you will encounter a virus. However, you should still take the threat of viruses seriously as they can do a great deal of damage. Always be careful about the files you allow into your computer and use virus checking software to check for infected files before you open them.

SEE ALSO...
● *Back up your work* *p82*

VIRUSES EXPLAINED
Find out what viruses are, why they exist, how they spread and what you can do to avoid them.

What are viruses?
Viruses are programs or segments of code that run without your knowledge. They are usually disguised and may sit on your computer for some time before activating. This gives them a chance to replicate or spread to programs, files and other connected computers before being discovered. There are all kinds of viruses, with different capabilities and methods of attack.

What can they do to my computer?
Some viruses are relatively harmless – for instance, they may cause a message to appear on your screen for no apparent reason. But other viruses aim to damage files so that you may lose some of your work or, worse still, they may damage vital Windows files, so you have to reinstall your system.

Who creates viruses and why?
Viruses are deliberately programmed by people who set out to spread them to as many computers as possible. There are many reasons why they do this. They could have political and ideological motives: a virus can be a protest against a government or market dominance. Or it might be an ego trip for someone who wishes to prove themselves as smarter than the software engineers.

How could I catch a virus?
Like a cold, a computer virus has to be caught, so it has to get into your PC from an external source. Such sources include:
External drives: If you often use CD-ROMs, DVDs or other removable discs, you could unwittingly open an infected file. A friend could give you a virus without even realising it.
The Web: You should download files from reputable sites only. Legitimate Web sites should state that they use anti-virus software to check all downloadable files and programs.
E-mail: The most common way to catch a virus is via an e-mail attachment. An attachment is a self-contained data file sent with an e-mail. When an e-mail includes an attachment, a paperclip is displayed beside the e-mail details (see below). Typically, you need to click on the paperclip to open and view the attachment. Only open an attachment if you know the person who sent it and are sure that they intended to send you the file.

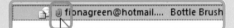

fionagreen@hotmail....   Bottle Brush

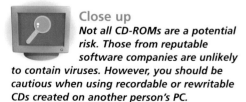

Close up
Not all CD-ROMs are a potential risk. Those from reputable software companies are unlikely to contain viruses. However, you should be cautious when using recordable or rewritable CDs created on another person's PC.

Watch out
E-mail is a popular vehicle for viruses but downloading an e-mail will not allow a virus to spread – you have to open the message or attachment. Unfortunately, most e-mail software automatically displays the contents of a message so, if you use e-mail, it is important to protect your system with anti-virus software.

TYPES OF VIRUS

Viruses take various forms and can attack your computer's files in different ways. Here are some of the main culprits.

File infector

This is a virus that attaches itself to program files. Program files are 'executable', which means that if you open the file, you launch a program. So if you don't open the file, the virus cannot run. Be suspicious of e-mail attachments or unverifiable downloads ending in '.exe', '.com', '.vbx' or '.bat', but also be aware that files created by programs such as Word and Excel could easily carry a macro virus. Windows will warn you about viruses when you start a download.

Boot sector virus

The boot sector contains files that tell your computer how to load the operating system each time you start up. If you insert a CD or DVD containing a boot sector virus into your computer, you will be able to read files on the disc without a problem. However, if you restart your PC with the CD still in the drive, your PC will access it, run the virus, and then may stop working. You should always avoid leaving a CD or DVD in the drive when you turn off your computer. Check your BIOS manual for information on boot sector virus protection.

Multipartite virus

Like file infectors, these viruses attach themselves to program files. When activated, they attack your hard drive's boot sector, so that the computer doesn't know how to find and load the operating system. This makes it impossible to start up your computer. Luckily, these viruses are hard to program and rare.

Macro virus

Some programs, such as Word and Excel, enable you to create macros, which are a series of instructions that you set up. Anyone with knowledge of the Visual Basic programming language can create a macro virus. If you open

a Word or Excel file containing a macro virus, it can spread to all your Word or Excel files. Macro viruses are not common these days and are easy to avoid as both Word and Excel display a box telling you macros are present when you open the file. Unless you're sure where they came from, click on the **Disable Macros** button.

Worm

A virus can replicate itself, but to move from computer to computer, the user has to pass on the infected file. Worms, on the other hand, can spread themselves. The famous worm trick is to e-mail itself to everyone in your Address Book. Computer networks are particularly vulnerable, as viruses can spread very quickly.

Trojan horse

These pretend to be harmless, even useful, applications. Then, when you least expect it, something nasty happens. Trojan horses are not classified as viruses because they cannot replicate themselves to infect other files on your computer.

Virus hoaxes

If you use e-mail, you are probably used to virus warnings. Unfortunately, it's hard to know when these are genuine and when they are just practical jokes. The danger of hoaxes is that you may start to ignore real warnings. Combat this by looking up the latest viruses on reputable Web sites, such as www.mcafee.com and www.symantec.com.

I Love You

In the year 2000, the infamous worm 'I Love You' brought computers and networks to a halt all over the world. It arrived as an e-mail file attachment called 'LOVE-LETTER-FOR-YOU.TEXT.vbs'. When the recipient opened the file, it read through the Address Book on that person's computer and forwarded itself to all the e-mail addresses it had read. Although it only affected Microsoft Outlook and Outlook Express, the 'I Love You' worm managed to spread around the world in a matter of hours, damaging data on millions of PCs and blocking up company networks with unwanted e-mails. The culprit was a young programmer in the Far East.

AVOIDING VIRUSES

There are many ways to safeguard your computer from being infected with a disruptive virus.

Anti-virus programs

These programs protect you against thousands of known viruses. The two best-known applications are McAfee Security Center and Norton AntiVirus from Symantec.

You can set up your anti-virus program to run in the background, so that it keeps regular checks on your computer and vets all incoming e-mails and external discs, such as CDs and DVDs.

Alternatively, you can run a virus check manually and choose exactly which drive and which files you want it to scan. Generally, the first place to look is the C: drive, where your operating system files are saved.

You've found a virus

When you run a virus scan, a log file documents the results. You can check this file at any time.

If your anti-virus program finds an infected file, you need to decide what to do with it. The file can be moved to a separate folder, deleted, or noted and left. Your program may be able to clean the file so that you can carry on using it. However, the safest option is to quarantine it.

Free updates

New viruses appear all the time, which is why the Web support provided by your software manufacturer is vital. Anti-virus programmers spend their working lives looking for viruses and creating fixes. Often you never hear about a virus because a fix is made before it spreads. Both McAfee and Symantec provide the latest anti-virus lists and software as automatic updates, similar to Windows Update. You can also sign up for e-mail newsletters, keeping you up to date on any new viruses for which fixes have not yet been created.

Better safe than sorry

Anti-virus software wards off most viruses, but there are additional steps you can take to keep your PC clean:

1 Keeping all of your software up to date helps to beat hackers. Microsoft sometimes issues patches for program loopholes on its Web site (see page 74). You should also check your other software manufacturers' Web sites regularly for updates and patches.

2 Back up your hard drive regularly (see page 82) and make sure you have the original discs for your programs and operating system.

If a virus infects your computer and you lose everything, you'll need to reinstall the software and all your data.

3 If you don't have the latest version of your anti-virus software, try an on-line virus-scanning service, such as HouseCall from Trend Micro (http.housecall.trendmicro.com/uk/).

4 Beware of e-mail attachments, even if they are from a friend. Avoid downloadable newsgroup files, and only download files from reputable Web sites.

5 Set up safety settings on your Web browser. For instance, you can choose to be prompted should you start to download a file by mistake. If you are using Internet Explorer, click on the **Tools** menu and select **Internet Options** and then the **Security** tab. Click on the **Custom Level** or **Default Level** buttons to adjust your settings, click on **OK**, and then on **OK** again.

Windows Defender

Vista comes with Windows Defender, a piece of anti-spyware software designed to detect and alert you when potentially malicious software is trying to install itself on your computer. When you use Windows Defender, it is important to have up-to-date definitions (a log of potential software threats). To help keep your definitions up to date, Windows Defender works with Windows Update (see page 74), to automatically install new definitions as they are released. To run Windows Defender, click on the **Start** button, **All Programs**, **Windows Defender** and then on **Scan**. You can schedule Windows Defender to run automatically. Click on **Tools**, **Options** and then, using the drop-down lists, set your automatic scanning preferences.

Troubleshooting

Getting help

If you encounter a problem with Windows – or you want to learn more about your hardware or software settings – consult Windows Vista's Help and Support facility. It contains definitions, step-by-step troubleshooters and Internet links for the latest information. If you need further assistance, there are plenty of other avenues to explore as well.

SEE ALSO...
- *Windows won't start up p94*
- *Error messages p96*

HELP AND SUPPORT

In most cases, you won't need to look any further than Windows' own Help and Support files to find the solution to your computer queries and problems.

Finding your way around

To access the Windows Help and Support resources, click on the **Start** button and select **Help and Support**. Information is arranged into general areas such 'Windows Basics' or 'Security and Maintenance', which are

represented by icons with headings underneath. Click on a heading to see a comprehensive list of related topics. Then click one of these topics to see a list of sub-topics. When you click on a

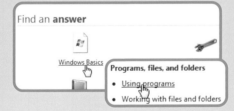

sub-topic, a Help article is displayed with a list of links to sections within the document so you

can quickly locate the exact information you are looking for.

If you get lost, the 'Home' button always returns you to the first window of Help and Support. The Back and Forward buttons help you navigate around the Help windows.

Expert advice

If a program designed to run under an older version of Windows doesn't work, you can run the Program Compatibility Wizard to make it run under Windows Vista. Open Help and Support, type 'compatible' in the Search box and click on **Start the Program Compatibility Wizard**.

Search help

If you don't find what you're looking for in the topics or contents list, use the 'Search' box. Click in the box and type a word or phrase and

press **Return**. The first 30 results will then be presented to you, with the best matches at the top of the list. Click on one of the entries. If

your computer is connected to the Internet, your searches can include the latest Help content from the 'Windows Assistance Online' Web site. Click on the **Offline Help** button at the bottom right of the window and select **Get online Help**.

Ask for assistance

If you can't solve your problem by using the self-help features already discussed, then you need further assistance. There are several ways you can achive this. Go to the **Start** menu and

click on **Help and Support**, or click on **Home** if it is already open. Click on **Windows Remote Assistance** then on **Invite someone you trust to help you**. You could also offer

your help to someone else. Now click on **Use e-mail to send an invitation**. (Note that if you use Web-based e-mail, you must save the invitation as a file and attach it to an e-mail.)

All communications in Remote Assistance are password controlled, so you will need to create a password. Click on **Next**. Your e-mail program will then open and create an invitation.

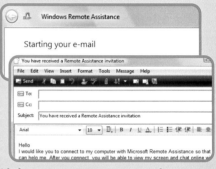

Links to more support options

Under the 'Ask someone' heading, click on **More support options** for more help:

- Use 'Windows Communities' to post questions and view answers.
- Contact Microsoft Customer Support for on-line technical assistance.
- Search the on-line 'Knowledge Base' for help with specific problems.
- For the latest information on problems, go to the 'Windows Help online'.

Close up
If you type two words in the Search box, the search returns a list of Help references which include both words. If you want to extend your search to include all references to each word, type the word 'or' between them.

Troubleshooters

When a feature does not work, Windows offers a specific type of help called a 'troubleshooter'. This asks you a series of in-depth questions that guide you step by step through the possible causes of the problem and help you to repair it. You can also go directly to the Troubleshooting section of Help and Support from the link on the 'Home' page. A list of Windows' troubleshooters will be displayed as text links in blue beneath a group heading. Subjects covered include using the Web, e-mail and hardware issues.

The Modem Troubleshooter

A common problem that is encountered when trying to connect to the Internet is your modem not being able to communicate with your ISP (Internet Service Provider). If this occurs, try the Modem Troubleshooter. It asks you to check whether your modem has been installed correctly, whether you are getting a dial tone (if

you have a dial-up connection), what the various settings are, and so on. It then takes you step by step through fixing the problem. If it doesn't solve the problem, the troubleshooter

Troubleshoot modem problems

Here are solutions to some common problems with using a dial-up modem to establish an Internet connection.

For information about establishing an Internet connection with a broadband modem, see Set up a DSL or cable connection.

▸ I can't get my modem to dial.

▸ I plugged my modem into a working phone line, but it's not able to dial a number.

▸ Windows does not seem to recognize my computer's internal modem.

▸ My computer has a software modem. Can I dial connections with a software modem the same way I would with a standard modem?

▸ My modem is connected to a working analog line, but it still can't dial a number.

▸ My modem is correctly installed, connected to a working analog phone line, and I've set up my dialing options, but it still can't dial a number.

advises you to contact the manufacturer, who will invariably ask you the same questions, so it's worth making a note of the answers while using the troubleshooter.

Following instructions

When using a Windows troubleshooter, it is important to answer all the questions and to carry out all the instructions on each page before clicking on the **Next** button to proceed. If you don't, you may carry out an inappropriate repair. If you make a mistake, click on **Back** to return to the previous question or, if you get stuck, click on the **Start Over** button to return to the beginning of the troubleshooter.

OTHER SOURCES OF HELP

Don't give up if Windows Help and Support hasn't provided you with the information you require. You can easily find more help in a host of other locations.

What's this?

Some dialogue boxes offer a handy localised help tool, identified by a question mark box in the top right-hand corner next to the 'Close' button.

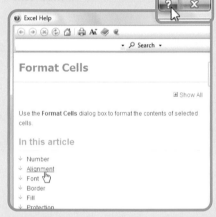

Click on the question mark, then on an item, and a dialogue box appears with information about the item.

Help with programs

Every program has a Help menu of its own. These usually operate in a similar way to Windows Help and Support, letting you

Close up
You can also get help on a problem by connecting to the Internet and typing a brief description of the problem in your Internet search engine. Try www.google.co.uk for useful links to help and assistance.

System information

To help diagnose the problem with your computer, technicians may ask you for details of your PC's system. To find this information, click on the **Start** button then on **All Programs**, **Accessories**, **System Tools** and finally **System Information**. On the left is a list of headings. Click on a heading to display information about it in the right pane.

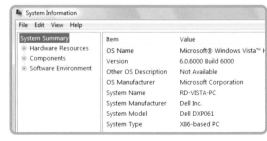

locate a topic through clickable links, an index or by typing in a keyword. Each of the

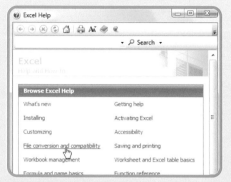

Microsoft Office programs offer extensive help, although it is advisable to get information from the Microsoft Web site, which is regularly updated. To access this information, you will need to be on-line.

Readme files
When you buy a program or get one free on a CD attached to the cover of a computer magazine, you will usually find that a text file called 'README' accompanies it. Locate this file using Windows' Search facility (see page 36) or

by browsing through the program's folder using Windows Explorer. Readme files usually explain new features not covered in the manual or Help file, or instructions on how to install the software properly. However, some Readme files include troubleshooting tips for problems discovered as a result of testing and running the program. To view a Readme file, double-click on it and it will open in Notepad, WordPad or Internet Explorer, depending on the type of file.

Calling for help
If all else fails, you may have to resort to asking for help. If you bought your computer equipment from a specialist shop, contact them first when things go wrong, particularly if it is still under guarantee. They might have come across your problem before and be able to offer a solution.

Alternatively, ask your PC manufacturer. Most have Web sites with detailed **FAQs** (Frequently Asked Questions), which might resolve the problem.

If you are having trouble connecting to the Internet, check that your service provider is not experiencing difficulties, then contact your modem manufacturer.

Contacting Microsoft
If you have recently upgraded to Windows Vista and are experiencing difficulties not covered by Help and Support, go to Microsoft's Support

Web site at http://support.microsoft.com. You'll find a large number of help topics under the headings 'Solution Centers' and 'Support Options'. Click on **Windows Vista**, in the left panel, to view the latest information on the operating system. If you can't find the answer you're after, click on **Contacts** and then on one of the links. Select your product in the next window and then go to 'E-mail' and 'Phone Support' details, where you will find contact information and charges. Click on **Sign In** using your Windows Live ID to start.

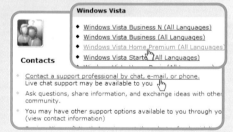

Key word
Almost every software Web site has a page of FAQs – Frequently Asked Questions – and their answers. Reading through FAQs can be a quick way to find solutions to problems. At the same time, you might also discover lots of other hints that will enhance the use of your computer.

Windows Live ID
Microsoft uses its Windows Live ID system to offer password-protected access to many services, including its on-line support centre. Once you have registered your details, you just have to sign in using your e-mail address and password. To sign up, go to https:// accountservices.passport.net.

Windows won't start up

Although Windows Vista is an extremely stable and reliable operating system, there are still times when it can let you down. Fortunately, Windows has a powerful repair tool called Startup Repair, on-line help facilities and interactive troubleshooter wizards to help you diagnose and fix problems. And if Windows won't run at all, you can start it in Safe Mode.

SEE ALSO...
- *Getting help p90*
- *System Restore p100*
- *Reinstalling Windows p102*

VISTA RECOVERY TOOL

Windows Vista has a recovery tool called Startup Repair, which can diagnose and fix many problems. If it can't, it will give you the necessary details to pass on to a specialist.

Startup Repair can fix many problems which might prevent Windows from starting up correctly, such as missing system files, drivers, boot configuration settings, or damaged registry settings and disk metadata (information about your hard disk). When you run Startup Repair it scans your computer for the problem. If a problem is identified, a troubleshooter will automatically launch and attempt to resolve the issue with little or no intervention from the user. If successful, the computer will reboot and an 'event' will be written and stored in the 'Event Viewer', providing information about the problem. If Startup Repair cannot repair the problem without user intervention, it will help you through the process to manually deal with the fault.

If Startup Repair is unsuccessful in its attempt to identify and fix the problem, it will restart the computer, reverting to the settings and configuration used before the problems occurred.

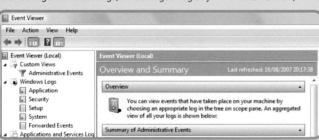

Starting up in Safe Mode
If you are able to start your computer but it doesn't run properly, restart it and press the F8 key before the Windows logo appears. Next,

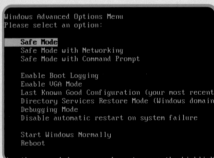

use the arrow keys to move through the menu and press **Return** when the 'Safe Mode' option is highlighted. Your PC should now start, with the words 'Safe Mode' in each corner of the screen, allowing you to use its diagnostic **tools.**

Close up
If you start your PC in Safe Mode you will not be able to access your printer and other external devices because the files needed to communicate with these devices will not be loaded.

Expert advice
Startup Repair cannot fix hardware failures, such as a faulty hard disk or incompatible memory. It's also not designed to protect against virus attacks or fix Windows installation problems. If you run Startup Repair and it is unsuccessful, a summary of the problem will be shown. A log of this and any earlier problems is held in Event Viewer (see p96).

Windows won't close down

Occasionally, you may find that your mouse pointer won't move, or that your keyboard doesn't seem to work. This is a problem known as 'freezing'. Fixing a frozen program is fairly simple because you can still access your Help and Support files. But if Windows freezes, you won't be able to use any of the menus or carry out normal program functions.

SEE ALSO...
- *Getting help* p90
- *System Restore* p100
- *Reinstalling Windows* p102

EMERGENCY SHUTDOWN

Often, when Windows freezes, normal commands can't be carried out. In this case you need to follow a special procedure to shut down.

When Windows 'hangs', you won't be able to restart by going to the Start menu as usual. Instead, press the **Ctrl + Shift + Esc** keys simultaneously. The Windows Task Manager will

open. Make sure the Applications tab is selected and you will see a list of the programs running when Windows froze. Shut each of them down and, if possible, save any changes by selecting each program in turn and clicking on **End Task**. A dialogue box appears asking if

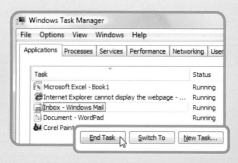

you want to save changes. Click on **Save**. If you had Internet Explorer open, close this last as it doesn't have active documents.

Closing programs in this way can sometimes unfreeze Windows. If it doesn't, then restarting Windows will usually do the trick.

Troubleshooting

Windows Vista is at the heart of your computer, underlying all the other programs you use. Because of this, the various options found

under Troubleshooting may need to shut down your PC in order to examine and correct the files that govern your system's operation.

Go to the **Start** button, click on **Help and Support** in the right panel, then click on **Troubleshooting**. Enter a keyword describing the problem you are having into the search box and press **Return**. It is good practice to familiarise yourself with the troubleshooting options in advance, before beginning the real process. You may find it helpful to print out the troubleshooting steps for later reference. If you have access to another PC that runs Windows Vista, you could follow the instructions on that PC as you examine your problem computer.

If all else fails

If you cannot shut down Windows by pressing the **Ctrl + Shift + Esc** keys, switch the PC off by pressing the Power button until it switches off. Wait 30 seconds and switch it on again.

Expert advice
If you always make sure that you shut down your computer correctly and that you properly uninstall applications you no longer use, you should be able to limit problems with the Windows operating system. Regular hard disk maintenance, such as Error-checking and Disk Defragmenter (see page 80) also help.

Close up
Where possible, restart or shut down your computer by clicking on the Start *button, then* Restart *or* Shut Down. ***This means that all Windows' settings are saved and each program closes properly before Windows shuts down.***

Error messages

Windows will usually warn you of a system or application problem by displaying an error message on your screen. These messages are there to help you and should never be ignored. Often, they not only describe the error, but suggest a reason for it and how to resolve it. Here are some of the most common error messages, and what you can do about them.

SEE ALSO...
- *Uninstall old programs p78*
- *Maintain your hard disk p80*
- *Back up your work p82*

MAKING SENSE OF MESSAGES

Here are some of the most common error messages. Find out what they mean and how to fix them.

'File in Use'
This message appears if you try to open a file that is already open in a different program. Either save and close the open file or select an option below, and click on **OK**.

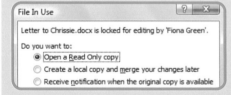

'Error Deleting File or Folder'
This message may appear if you try to delete a file that is still open. Check through the open files on your Taskbar, close the one you want to delete and then drag it to the Recycle Bin.

Missing or out-of-date files
This message appears if you have deleted or renamed a file and then tried to open it from your 'recent files' list. Alternatively, a file may have been overwritten or deleted while a program was installed.

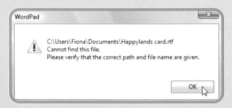

Error-checking messages
Windows' built-in maintenance tools include an error-checking utility that checks your hard disk

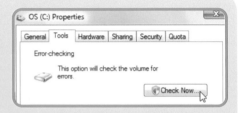

for problems and attempts to fix them. If it detects and reports errors it cannot fix, you should contact your PC dealer.

'File Corruption'
If one of your files has become corrupted, the only option is to delete it, and replace it with your back-up copy (see page 82).

Use Event Viewer
Event Viewer is a diagnostic tool that runs in the background and logs information about hardware and software problems. While the tool cannot remedy the problems, the information can be useful when discussing the issues with a PC engineer. Go to the **Start** button, click on **Control Panel**, double-click on **Administrative Tools**, then double-click on **Event Viewer**. Under the 'Level' column, entries for serious problems are displayed with an '!' in a red circle, warnings appear with an '!' in a yellow triangle, and information entries have an 'i' in a blue circle.

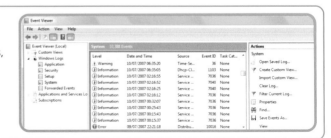

Program crashes

When a program crashes, your mouse pointer turns into an hourglass icon and you won't be able to type or access any of the menus. If this is the case, you will need to exit the program and you may lose work that hasn't been saved. Some crashes may just be momentary glitches, but if they reoccur regularly, you should reinstall the program.

SEE ALSO...
- *Maintain your hard disk* *p80*
- *Back up your work* *p82*
- *Getting help* *p90*

BEFORE YOU START
*Try clicking on the red Close Program button at the top right of your program window. If this doesn't work, press **Alt + F4**. If this also fails, follow the steps below.*

1 You'll know when a program has crashed because you won't be able to use its menus. However, if you move the mouse away from the program window, you may find it reverts from an hourglass to a pointer. Press the **Ctrl + Shift + Esc** keys. This key combination opens the Windows Task Manager box, which lists all the programs running on your PC. Select the program that is not responding and click on the **End Task** button.

2 If the program closes, exit the Task Manager, launch the program again and resume working.

If the Task Manager can't close the program, another dialogue box will open. In the new dialogue box, click on **End Now** to close the program. If you have to do this, you should restart Windows.

Occasionally, more than one program may crash.

If this happens, you should close each program in turn. Unsaved work in any of the programs will be lost.

Sometimes Windows may issue a message, such as 'Microsoft Office Word has stopped working'. If this occurs you have no option but to click on **Close program**. Wherever possible, Windows will notify you if a solution to the problem is available.

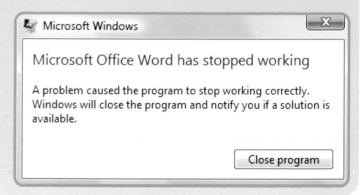

Close up
To reduce the risk of losing data in a crash, some programs allow you to save data automatically at set intervals. In Word, click on the Office button and then on Word Options. Click on Save in the left pane and select a time in the 'Save AutoRecover information every…' box. Click on OK.

CHECKING FOR PROBLEM SOLUTIONS

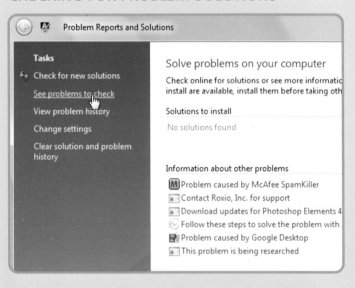

1 When a program stops working, Windows creates a report so that you can check for a solution. Go to the **Start** button and click on **Control Panel**, then double-click on **Problem**

Reports and Solutions. Any solutions found will be listed under 'Solutions to install'. Click on **See problems to check** in the left pane to display all problems recorded but not yet reported.

2 Windows will then display the product, type of problem and the date and time the software stopped working. Click on **View details** in the

last column to find out more. Click on the tick box next to a recorded problem, then on **Check for solutions**. Windows will then search for a solution.

Reinstalling a problem program

If a program persistently crashes, you should uninstall it. Go to the **Start** button, click on **Control Panel** and then, under 'Programs', click on **Uninstall a program**. Select the relevant program from the list and follow the on-screen instructions. Restart your PC and install the program from scratch by placing the program's installation disk in the drive. If the program doesn't install automatically, click on the **Start** button, select **Computer**, and then double-click on the CD/DVD drive icon. A warning message will appear. Click on **Allow** to confirm that the PC should access the program. Finally, click on 'Setup' or a similar start icon or link.

Key word
Temporary files store information about a program currently in use and are usually deleted automatically when you close the program that created them. However, if the PC crashes they remain on your hard disk and must be deleted manually.

CLEARING OUT TEMPORARY FILES

1 To make your PC run more smoothly, use Disk Cleanup to remove unnecessary files on your hard drive. Click on the **Start** button and select **All Programs**, then **Accessories**. Select **System Tools** and click on **Disk Cleanup**. A dialogue box appears, with your hard disk (normally C:) selected. Click on **OK**. Disk Cleanup then calculates how much space can be made available.

2 In the Disk Cleanup dialogue box put a tick in the box next to 'Temporary files'. Look through the other options to see if there is anything else you would like to clear from your hard drive, then click on **OK**. In the next box, click on **Delete Files** to confirm you would like to permanently delete the files. Disk Cleanup will then delete these files. A panel shows the progress.

System Restore

Occasionally a computer will develop a problem immediately after new software or hardware has been installed. If the problem proves difficult to resolve, it is possible to retrieve your previous working setup by using the Windows Vista System Restore feature. This tool effectively winds back the clock to a time when your PC was running smoothly.

SEE ALSO...

● *Uninstall old programs p78*

BEFORE YOU START
System Restore will help you return your PC to good health.

*Click on the **Start** menu and select **All Programs, Accessories, System Tools** and then **System Restore**.*

Restore system files and settings

System Restore can help fix problems that might be making you computer run slowly or stop responding.

System Restore does not affect any of your documents, picture other personal data, and the process is reversible. How does S Restore work?

⦿ Recommended restore:

Select this option to undo the most recent update, driv or software installation if you think it is causing problem

05/09/2007 08:18:06 Install: Windows Update

Current time zone: GMT Daylight Time

○ Choose a different restore point

To create a restore point, open System Protection.

< Back   Next >

1 In the System Restore dialogue box, you need to choose between 'Recommended restore' – the most recent restore point – and 'Choose a different restore point'. Make your selection and click on **Next**.

2 If you chose 'Recommended restore', just click on **Finish** to begin the restore. If you want a different restore point, you will be presented with a list of options showing the date, time and a brief description of the restore point. If none of these are suitable, click in the box next to 'Show restore points older than 5 days' and click on **Next**.

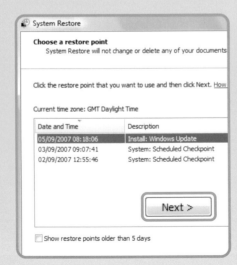

System Restore

Choose a restore point
    System Restore will not change or delete any of your documents

Click the restore point that you want to use and then click Next. How

Current time zone: GMT Daylight Time

Date and Time	Description
05/09/2007 08:18:06	Install: Windows Update
03/09/2007 09:07:41	System: Scheduled Checkpoint
02/09/2007 12:55:46	System: Scheduled Checkpoint

Next >

☐ Show restore points older than 5 days

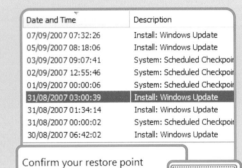

Date and Time	Description
07/09/2007 07:32:26	Install: Windows Update
05/09/2007 08:18:06	Install: Windows Update
03/09/2007 09:07:41	System: Scheduled Checkpoin
02/09/2007 12:55:46	System: Scheduled Checkpoin
01/09/2007 00:00:06	System: Scheduled Checkpoin
31/08/2007 03:00:39	Install: Windows Update
31/08/2007 01:34:14	Install: Windows Update
31/08/2007 00:00:02	System: Scheduled Checkpoin
30/08/2007 06:42:02	Install: Windows Update

Confirm your restore point

Time: 31/08/2007 03:00:39 (GMT D

Description: Install: Windows Update

Finish

3 If you chose from the most recent list, click on **Finish**. If you chose 'Show restore points older than 5 days', select a date from the new list, click on **Next** and then on **Finish**. You will see a warning message informing you that, once started, System Restore may not be interrupted until after it has completed. Click on **Yes** to continue. A progress bar displays during the restore. When the restore is complete, your PC will restart.

SYSTEM RESTORE

By undoing certain changes you have made to your computer after a chosen date, System Restore can return your troubled PC to a healthy state.

Windows is capable of achieving this rolling back of time because it regularly creates snapshots of your computer's operating system called 'restore points'. System Restore records the system files and drivers on your PC at given times so that it knows how to return your PC to a state before it stopped working properly.

Automatic restore points

Windows automatically records an initial restore point when it is first launched. After that, it creates restore points at regular intervals. System restore points are also created whenever you install a new program or a Windows automatic update.

Creating your own restore point

If you are about to change your PC's settings or clear out some files and you're worried that you might destabilise your computer – for example, if you are installing a new piece of hardware – create your own restore point before you start. That way you know that, whatever you do, you will be able to return your system to its current working state. To do this, open the System Restore Wizard by clicking on the **Start** button and selecting **All Programs**, **Accessories**, **System Tools**, and then **System Restore**.

To create a restore point, open System Protection.

Click on **open System Protection** and then, in the next box, click on **Create**. Give your new restore point a description that will remind you why you created it – you might use the name of

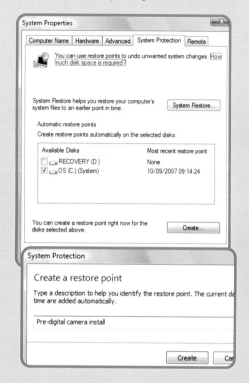

your new installation, for example – and click on **Create**. A progress bar displays as the

restore point is created, and a completion message is displayed at the end of the process.

If it all goes wrong

If you are not happy with your PC after restoring it to an earlier state, System Restore can easily

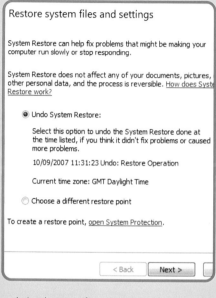

undo its changes. If you have completed a restoration very recently, an extra option to **Undo System Restore** appears when you open the System Restore function. Select it and click on **Next** to proceed. Alternatively, you can select **Choose a different restore point**, click on **Next**, and select a restore point prior to the restoration date you previously chose.

Close up
Any files in your Documents folder and data files created between the rollback date and the present will be left unchanged – only system files, programs and drivers are removed by System Restore.

Bright idea
If your PC develops a problem after you have installed a new program, try uninstalling the software in the normal way, using Uninstall a program (see page 78), before restoring your computer's system.

Reinstalling Windows

Sometimes you will encounter persistent problems with Windows. If you have tried all other remedies, the only solution is to reinstall. This restores the operating system files but leaves your work and programs unaffected. It is advisable to run Error-checking and Disk Defragmenter before reinstalling to help prevent problems occurring during installation.

SEE ALSO...
- *Maintain your hard disk* *p80*
- *Windows won't start up* *p94*
- *Program crashes* *p97*

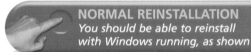

NORMAL REINSTALLATION
You should be able to reinstall with Windows running, as shown here. If you can't get Windows to start at all, see 'Starting without Windows' opposite.

1 Insert your Windows Vista disc into your PC's CD/DVD drive. The disc should run automatically and start to take you through the installation process. A window opens asking if you want to either 'Check compatibility online' or 'Install now'. Click on **Install now** to replace Windows on your PC with an unmodified version.

2 The Vista installation program will examine your computer and automatically collect all the information it needs to work out the best configuration. If you are connected to the Internet, it will access the Microsoft Web site for any appropriate Vista updates that have recently been released. It is advisable to download any updates to keep your PC secure and running smoothly.

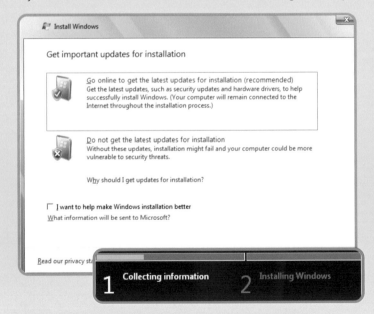

Starting without Windows

If Windows won't start up, you can put your Windows Vista disc in the drive and try to start your PC using that. Insert it into your CD/DVD drive and switch your PC off. Then switch it back on again to start your system from the Windows Vista disc. You can then go to the installation menu and select the 'Repair Your Computer' option to try to correct the fault.

Some older PCs may not support start-up from the CD/DVD, in which case you will not be able to use the Vista DVD as a rescue disc. If this is the case, you should consult an expert.

Watch out
Only reinstall Windows if System Restore (see page 100) did not resolve the problem. Always back up your data first (see page 80) and bear in mind that all programs and Windows updates will need to be reinstalled as well. If your PC came with a 'recovery disc', use that instead of reinstalling – follow the manufacturer's instructions.

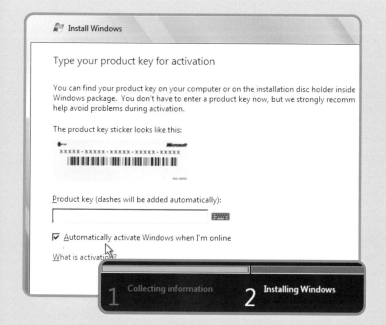

4 A large proportion of the installation time is spent copying vital Windows files to your PC. The time this takes depends on the speed of your CD/DVD drive, your hard drive and on the speed of your computer. You must wait for the full installation to complete. A 'Thank you' message screen will then appear, containing a 'Start' button. Click on **Start** to restart your PC.

3 You will now be asked for your 'product key'. This can be found on the sleeve of your Windows Vista installation disc. If your PC was purchased with Vista pre-loaded, your supplier should have given you this information. Check the box next to 'Automatically activate Windows when I'm online'. Click on **Next** to continue.

GLOSSARY

A

A: On older PCs, the drive used for floppy disks.

Accessories Small programs, such as Calculator or Notepad, which are included with Windows.

Active window The window you are working in. To make a window active, click on it and it will 'jump' to the front. *See Window.*

ADSL Asymmetric Digital Subscriber Line. A way of getting broadband Internet access through a normal telephone line. *See Broadband.*

Aero New ways of viewing open windows with Vista, with a 3D display and 'thumbnails' above the file name shown on the Taskbar.

Alt A key on the keyboard that activates a command when pressed in combination with other keys.

Application A piece of software designed to perform specific tasks. Also known as a program.

Archive To transfer files to a separate system, such as a CD-R. *See Backup.*

Arrow keys *See Cursor keys.*

Attachment A file sent with an e-mail message.

Audio file A digital sound recording. Windows audio files usually have '.wma' after the file name.

B

Backup A duplicate of a file or folder, made in case of loss or damage to the original data.

Backups are usually made on removable discs, such as CDs.

BIOS Basic Input/Output System. Instructions that control the communication between a PC and its hardware at a basic level.

Bit The smallest unit of computer storage, with a value of 1 or 0. 'Bit' is a contraction of 'binary digit'. All computers use the binary system to process data.

Bitmap An on-screen image made up of tiny dots or pixels. *See Pixels.*

Broadband High-speed Internet access via either an ADSL, cable or satellite connection. *See ADSL.*

Boot or **boot up** To switch on the PC, activating the BIOS.

Bug An error or fault in a program which can cause it to malfunction or crash, possibly leading to data loss.

Button An on-screen image that, when clicked on with the mouse, performs a function. For example, the 'OK' or 'Yes' buttons that confirm a proposed course of action.

Byte A unit of computer memory, made up of eight bits. One byte of memory stores the code for a single character, such as a letter of the alphabet.

C

C: Also called the 'C drive', this letter represents a PC's hard disk, on which all programs and documents are stored.

Cache A section of high-speed memory or disk space allocated to storing recently used data, thus

increasing the speed at which that data can be accessed again.

CD-ROM Compact Disc–Read Only Memory. A storage device in the form of a CD, containing up to 700MB of data. Most software comes on CD-ROMs, which are inserted into the PC and usually accessed from the 'D drive'.

CD-R/CD-RW Compact Disc Recordable/Rewritable. CDs that can be written to, using a special type of disc drive (sometimes called a 'burner'). CD-Rs can only be written to once; CD-RWs can be rewritten many times over.

Chip A tiny circuit that processes or stores data. A processor chip carries out calculations and a memory chip stores data.

Click To press and release the left mouse button once. This is how menu and dialogue box options and toolbar buttons are selected.

Clipboard A virtual location where anything cut or copied is stored. The Windows Clipboard stores one piece of data at a time. A new cut or copied item will overwrite previous material on the Clipboard. Use the Paste command to insert a Clipboard item in a document.

CMOS Complementary Metal Oxide Semiconductor. A memory chip that stores your PC's BIOS configuration settings and the date and time.

Compression A means of reducing the size of files so they use less storage space and can be copied or downloaded quickly.

Computer An option found in the Start menu of a PC running Windows Vista. Select it to access

everything stored in the system on the hard drive and CD/DVD drive.

Configuration The settings used to make sure your hardware and software run as you want them to.

Control key The two 'Ctrl' keys on the same row as the Space bar that can activate commands or shortcuts when pressed with other keys.

Control Panel A range of utility programs that enable you to control your Windows settings. For example, you can change the way your Desktop looks, add new hardware, or alter your PC's sound scheme.

Copy To make a duplicate of a file, folder, image, or part of a document.

CPU Central Processing Unit. The 'brain' of your PC, which carries out millions of arithmetic and control functions every second. Its power is defined by its speed in MegaHertz (MHz), or GigaHertz (GHz) – the number of times it makes a decision every second. For example, an 800MHz CPU carries out 800 million calculations per second.

Crash A program or operating system failure. Your PC has crashed if the screen 'freezes' and the keyboard or mouse commands do not work. You may need to restart the computer.

Cursor A marker, usually a flashing vertical line, indicating where any item typed, or inserted, will appear on the page.

Cursor keys The four arrow keys at the bottom right of the keyboard that move the insertion point or allow you to scroll through a window's contents.

Cut To remove selected files, folders, text or images to the Clipboard, where they are stored for later use.

D

D: The CD/DVD drive on a PC. In speech, it is referred to as the 'D' drive. *See CD-ROM* and *DVD*.

Data Information processed or stored digitally on a computer.

Database A system for storing information so it can be easily accessed, organised and sorted. Each entry is called a 'record', and each category in a record is called a 'field'.

Default Settings and preferences automatically adopted by your PC when no others have been specified by the user.

Defragmenter A program that 'tidies' files on the hard disk. Occasionally Windows splits up a file when it is being saved so the file elements become fragmented. This makes retrieving the file slower. The Defragmenter regroups related data.

Delete To completely remove a selected file, folder, or image, or a piece of text from your document.

Desktop The screen displayed when Windows has finished starting up. Any icons on screen, together with the Taskbar and Start button, are known collectively as the Desktop. *See Icon* and *Taskbar.*

Dialogue box A window that displays messages from the operating system or the program currently in use. This usually asks for confirmation of a proposed course of action or for information to be input by the user.

Digital image An image which is stored in binary format, so it can be viewed and changed on a PC.

Disk A device for storing digital information. A hard disk is made of a stack of rigid disks, known as 'platters'.

Disk cleanup A program that will find and delete errors on your hard disk, freeing up memory.

Disk tools Programs that manage and maintain the data on the hard disk, making sure that it can be stored and retrieved efficiently.

Document A single piece of work created in a program, also referred to as a 'file'.

Documents A folder option found in the Start menu. Each user has a Documents folder for their files.

DOS Disk Operating System. Usually used to refer to the operating system for PCs before Windows.

Dots per inch (dpi) The number of dots per square inch that either make up an image on screen or that a printer has the capability to print. The more dots, the greater the detail and quality of the image.

Double-click To press and release the left mouse button twice in quick succession.

Download To copy files or programs from the Internet or from another computer to your own. You 'download' e-mail to read it.

Drag A mouse action used to select text, reshape objects, or to move an object or file. Click and keep the left button down. Then move the mouse as required and release.

Drive A device that holds a disk. A drive has a motor that spins the disk, and a head that reads and writes to it, in a similar way to the heads in a cassette deck.

Driver Software that enables communication between Windows and a hardware device, such as a printer or modem.

DVD Digital Versatile Disc or Digital Video Disc. A disc the same size as a CD but with a much larger storage capacity, up to 17GB. Because of this, DVDs can store whole movies with different languages, subtitles and extra footage.

E

E-mail Electronic mail. Messages that are sent from one computer to another using the Internet or any network.

Error message A small window on screen warning that a fault has occurred and possibly suggesting action to remedy it.

Expansion card Add-on hardware, which fits into a PC and expands its capabilities, such as a soundcard.

External hardware Additional computer equipment attached by cable to a PC, such as a printer.

F

Field An area of a database that contains a category of information, such as 'Name'.

File Any item that is stored on a computer, whether it is a program, a document, or an image.

File extension A three or four letter code assigned to the end of a file name when it is saved. This indicates the type of file so Windows knows which program to open it in. Also known as a suffix.

File format The way in which files created by different programs are saved. File formats are indicated by a code at the end of the file name. *See File extension.*

Firewall Software or hardware that limits the access that can be gained to your PC through an Internet connection.

Flash drive Small, portable storage device used for easily transferring files from one PC to another.

Folder A virtual storage location for files and programs.

Font A specific style and set of characters for a typeface, for example, Times New Roman.

Format (disks) To prepare a disk for storing and retrieving data for a specific operating system.

Format (documents) To alter a document's appearance, using style, typography and layout options.

Freeware Programs which cost nothing and are often available to download from the Internet.

Function keys The 12 F keys running across the top of the keyboard, ranging from F1 to F12, which perform special tasks depending on the program.

G

.gif file Graphics Interchange Format. A file format for digital images used on Web sites.

Gigabyte (GB) A unit of memory capacity. One gigabyte consists of 1024 megabytes (MB).

H

Hard disk A computer's storage device containing the operating system, programs and all files. It is sometimes referred to as the 'C drive' or 'hard drive'.

Hardware The physical parts of a computer, including the system unit, monitor and keyboard.

Highlight To select text, images or cells by dragging the cursor over the item. See *Drag*.

I

Icon A graphical representation of a file or a function, for example, the Recycle Bin icon on the Desktop.

Import To bring text, images or files from one program into another.

Inkjet printer A printer that works by squirting tiny drops of ink onto the surface of the paper. Many home printers work in this way.

Install To copy a program's files onto the hard disk and set it up ready for use. Programs are usually installed from CD-ROMs.

Internet A contraction of 'International Network'. It consists of millions of computers around the world, which are linked by phone and cable lines.

ISP Internet Service Provider. A company that provides a connection from your computer to the Internet.

J

.jpeg Joint Photographics Experts Group. A file format that compresses images so they take up less storage space on your hard disk.

K

Keyboard shortcut A group of keys pressed simultaneously as a quick way of issuing a command.

Kilobyte (KB) A unit of data capacity. One kilobyte equals 1024 bytes. *See Gigabyte, Megabyte and Terabyte.*

Kilobytes per second (kbps) A measurement for the speed with which data can be sent to or from a computer via a modem.

L

Laptop A portable computer with a keyboard and flat screen.

Laser printer A type of printer that uses a laser to draw images electrostatically onto a drum and then transfers them to paper.

Log on To access a computer, file or Web site using a security procedure, such as a password.

M

Maximise To increase the size of a window to fill the entire screen.

Media Center Alternative to Media Player that can also give access to TV and FM radio.

Media Player Windows program for managing digital files, such as pictures, music and DVDs.

Megabyte (MB) A unit of memory capacity. One megabyte equals 1024 kilobytes.

Memory Computer chips that store data. *See RAM and ROM.*

Menu bar A bar at the top of a window containing lists of options arranged by category. Click on a heading to see a drop-down menu of options.

Minimise To reduce a window to a button on the Taskbar.

Modem A device that enables your computer to connect to the Internet. It converts a computer's digital signals into analog signals that can be transmitted over phone lines.

Monitor A piece of equipment that displays all your work on screen. This may work in a similar way to a TV screen or may be a flat monitor made up of thousands of tiny transistors.

Motherboard The circuit board on which the central processing unit (CPU), memory, and slots for expansion cards are mounted.

Mouse pointer A small arrow or cursor on screen controlled by the mouse. Pointers can be a pointing hand, a pen or a cross, depending on the program and the action.

Multimedia Computing that can combine audio, graphics, text and video.

Music The default file for storing music files in Windows Vista.

N

Network Interconnected computers (including other hardware) that share files and resources.

O

Open To bring a file, folder or program into use.

Operating system (OS) Software that controls the running of a computer. Microsoft Windows is the most popular OS for PCs.

P

Paste To insert a file, folder, text or data that has been cut or copied.

PC-compatible Software or hardware that works on a PC.

PCI slot A connector inside a PC into which you can fit circuit boards, such as a soundcard.

Peripheral A device, such as a scanner, that can be connected to a PC but is not central to its operation.

Pictures The default folder in Windows Vista for storing photographs and other images.

Pixels Individual dots on a screen. The number of pixels determines the level of detail and quality of display.

Plug and play Where extra items can be added to your PC without the need for loading new software.

Plug-ins Hardware or software that adds extra functionality. Web sites often provide plug-ins for visitors to download, so that they can view all the content.

Port A socket at the back of a computer for connecting devices.

Processor The central processing unit (CPU) of a PC.

Program Software that interacts with the computer's hardware allowing the user to perform specific tasks.

Properties The attributes of a file or folder, such as its creation date, format and author's name.

R

RAM Random Access Memory. Memory chips used for temporary storage of information, such as the currently active file. As soon as the computer is switched off, this temporary information disappears.

Recycle Bin A Desktop feature used to store files ready for permanent deletion.

Registry The Windows database of its configuration settings and installed programs.

Reset button A button on the system unit, usually below the power button, which allows users to restart their PC if it 'crashes'.

Resolution The degree of detail on a screen or a printed document, measured in dots per inch (dpi). The higher the dpi, the better the detail.

Right-click To press and release the right mouse button once.

ROM Read Only Memory. Memory chips that are used for storing basic PC details.

Run command A Windows feature that allows you to launch a program by typing in its name.

S

Save To store or copy a document to a disk.

Save As Allows a file to be saved using a different name, drive or format, without affecting the original saved version.

Scanner A device which converts images and text to a digital format so they can be manipulated and reproduced by a computer. *See Digital image.*

Screensaver A picture or animation that appears on screen when the PC is left idle for a specified time.

Scroll To move through the contents of a window or menu vertically or horizontally.

Search A utility that searches a range of files for specified data, or which searches the hard disk for files or folders.

Search engines Databases on the Internet, which you can use to locate Web sites by typing in a key word or phrase.

Select To click on a file, folder, image, text, or other item, so it can be manipulated.

Shortcut An icon that provides quick access to a file, folder or program stored on the hard disk. A shortcut icon looks identical to the icon of the item to which it is linked but has a small overlaid arrow in the bottom left corner.

Software Programs that allow users to perform specific functions; Microsoft Excel and Microsoft Word are examples of software.

Software suite A collection of programs in a single package, for example, Microsoft Office.

Soundcard A device that lets users record, play and edit sound files. It fits into an expansion slot on the motherboard.

Sound file An audio file. To hear it, double-click on the file (you will need speakers and a soundcard).

Start button The button to the left of the Taskbar, which accesses the 'Start' menu.

Status bar Strip at the bottom of a program window that displays information on the open document.

System files Windows' vital operating files.

System unit The PC box, containing the hard disk, the processor, memory, and sockets for peripheral devices, such as a printer.

T

Tab key A key (next to Q on the keyboard) used to tabulate text, to move between cells in spreadsheets, or to move from one database field to the next.

Taskbar A bar along the bottom of the screen that displays the Start button and buttons for all programs and documents currently open.

Template A document containing preset basic elements, which can be used as the basis for other documents.

Terabyte A unit of memory capacity. A single terabyte is 1024 gigabytes.

TFT (Thin Film Transistor) A type of LCD (Liquid Crystal Display) screen used on laptop computers and flat-screen monitors.

Tile To reduce the size of a group of open windows, arranging them so they can all be seen at once.

Toolbar A bar or small window, which contains buttons and drop-down lists for issuing commands or accessing functions.

U

Uninstall To remove programs from the PC's hard disk.

Upgrade To improve the performance or specification of a PC by adding new hardware, such as a higher capacity disk drive.

USB Universal Serial Bus. A hardware connector that allows users to plug a number of devices into their PCs.

Utilities Software that assists in housekeeping or troubleshooting computer functions.

V

View A menu category containing options that change the way a file is displayed on screen.

Virus A program designed to damage a computer system.

W

WiFi Popular name for IEEE 802.11b, a standard for wireless networks suitable for use in the home.

Window The self-contained viewing and working area of a folder or program. Several windows can be open at once on the Desktop.

Windows An operating system for PCs, which allows users to run many programs at once, opening individual files called 'windows'.

Windows Explorer A program for viewing the contents of a PC's disks in a single window.

Windows Live Messenger An on-line means of instant communication.

Wizard A program tool that guides users through a complex task.

Word processing Text-based operations carried out on the PC, such as letter writing.

World Wide Web The part of the Internet, composed of millions of linked Web pages, which can be viewed using Web browsing software, such as Internet Explorer.

Z

Zipped folder A special Windows folder that compresses files when they are placed in it. They are identified by a zip on the folder icon.

INDEX

Numbers shown in **bold** type are for main references to the subject listed

How to do just about anything in Microsoft® Windows® Vista™

was edited and designed by The Reader's Digest Association Limited, London

First edition copyright © 2008
The Reader's Digest Association Limited,
11 Westferry Circus, Canary Wharf, London E14 4HE.
www.readersdigest.co.uk

We are committed both to the quality of our products and the service we provide to our customers. We value your comments, so please do contact us on **08705 113366**, or via our Web site at **www.readersdigest.co.uk**
If you have any comments or suggestions about this book, e-mail us at **gbeditorial@readersdigest.co.uk**

Origination: Colour Systems Limited, London

Printing and binding: CT Printing, China

Book code 400-367 UP0000-1
ISBN 978 0 276 44269 8
Oracle code 250011971H.00.24